REIMAGINI BLACK ART CRIMINOLOGY

A New Criminological Imagination

Martin Glynn

BRISTOL
UNIVERSITY
PRESS

First published in Great Britain in 2021 by

Bristol University Press
University of Bristol
1-9 Old Park Hill
Bristol
BS2 8BB
UK
t: +44 (0)117 954 5940
e: bup-info@bristol.ac.uk

Details of international sales and distribution partners are available at bristoluniversitypress.co.uk

© Bristol University Press 2021

British Library Cataloguing in Publication Data
A catalogue record for this book is available from the British Library

ISBN 978-1-5292-1392-8 hardcover
ISBN 978-1-5292-1393-5 paperback
ISBN 978-1-5292-1394-2 ePub
ISBN 978-1-5292-1395-9 ePdf

Cover design: Liam Roberts
Front cover image: GettyImages-1249641728

Contents

Note on Terminology

The term 'black' used in this book represents a unity of experiences, in relation to racism, white supremacy, and racialized oppression, among people whose skin is not white. The term 'black' is not static but changes over time, both within and between groups. I also want to recognize indigenous positions as a way of transcending the binary of the Global North–South divide, who may not identify with the term 'black', but are connected through a history of racial subjugation and oppression. Similarly, the terms 'black art' and 'black arts' used throughout this book are interchangeable, located within the context laid down by each chapter.

About the Author

Dr Martin Glynn is a criminologist, dramatist, poet, children's author, and data storyteller, with over four decades of experience of working in criminal justice, public health, and educational settings. He has a Cert Ed, a Master's degree in criminal justice policy and practice, and gained his PhD at Birmingham City University in February 2013, where he is currently a lecturer in criminology. Dr Glynn's previous books include *Black Men, Invisibility, and Desistance from Crime: Towards a Critical Race Theory from Crime* (Routledge, 2014), and *Speaking Data and Telling Stories: Data Verbalization for Researchers* (Routledge, 2019).

Acknowledgements

To my amazing mother, Jill Glynn (RIP), who encouraged me to dream, explore, be curious, and, more importantly, aim for the stars. To my stepfather, Ted who ensured that I understood the value of both reading and writing. To my good friend and constant support, Kathryn Russell-Brown for her campaigning work around the need for a 'black' criminology, which provided the impetus for this book. To James Unnever, Shaun Gabbidon, and Cecelia Chouhy, for their seminal book *Building a Black Criminology* (Routledge, 2020). To Professors James Thompson, Shadd Maruna, Fergus McNeil, and Ross Deuchar, for their unwavering academic support over the years. To my inner circle, Dr Mohammed Rahman, Craig Pinkney, Ray Douglas, Tanayah Sam, and numerous others who have been there for me, regardless. To the new generation of young scholar-activists – Malieka, Rami, Jade, Asante, Natasha, Kerisha, Naomi, Darren, Janet, Michelle, and Caprice – whose texts, phone calls, and constant love, has never wavered. To my good friend and colleague Andrea, from the National Justice Museum, who reignited my passion for being all things curious and creative. To my dear friend and colleague, Vinette, who sadly passed away, who always saw and supported the potential in my ideas around bringing art and academia together. To my tight bredrin Richard, whose unstinting support and belief in me has been the oil that has run my engine. To one of my oldest of friendships, Andrew, 40 years in total, to whom I owe a debt of friendship, love, and loyalty. To those countless artists, offenders, and community people who have always been encouraging and supportive of my 'out the box' thinking. To my close friends, allies, and enemies for giving me a massive dose of courage to continue the passion for my work. To my family, children, grandchildren, and great grandson for giving me the reason for continuing with my legacy work. To the staff at Bristol

University Press who, from its inception, saw the value and potential of the vision behind the book, and supported me unconditionally. And, finally, to my exceptional wife Jennifer, who has had to suffer my rants, moans, gripes, as well as putting up with the turmoil that ensues when writing a book such as this.

This caged bird has finally sung.

Preface

First, I would like to say thank you to those who have purchased my book, as I hope you will take from its contents what you need. Writing *Reimagining Black Art and Criminology* has been a troubling, evocative, and humbling experience in equal measure. However, at a time when increased right-wing populism continues to undermine progressive ideas about racial parity, I was constantly reminded that the struggle is far from over and must continue. Undeterred by this state of affairs, my new book seeks to bring urgent attention to a provocative criminological perspective viewed through the lens of 'black art'. To the cynics, critics, and race deniers, I say "welcome". Exploring the arts and creativity in relation to crime and its formations is not a new phenomenon. O'Brien (2008) connects Victorian poetry to developments in the Victorian discourse on crime. Jacobsen (2014) provides a context to reconsider and reimagine how criminological knowledge may be creatively, poetically constructed, obtained, corroborated, and applied. Saleh-Hanna (2010), similarly, sees black resistance through the use of music. Zoboi and Salaam (2020) have also written a novel in verse about a black boy who is wrongfully incarcerated. In essence, what I am putting forward here is not new, but instead is part of a continuum of art-infused criminological thinking and expression. The need for revision of our current thinking using creative means is upon us. Hartney and Vuong (2009) see non-white peoples across the world as being alarmingly overrepresented in the criminal justice system. While Lammy (2017) asserts that if the agencies of the criminal justice system cannot provide evidence-based understandings of racial disparities, then reforms should be introduced to address this differential racialization of crime and its formations. Ferell (2014) argues that criminology remains largely a self-perpetuating practice that lacks the ability to look outside itself. Ferell further points out that: 'Criminology today is crippled by its own methodology, its potential for analysis, critique and appreciation lost within a welter of survey forms, governmental data sets and statistical manipulations' (2014: 285). Travis et al (2005) see the unprecedented levels of incarceration and re-entry for black offenders as having widespread and poorly understood consequences for their families and the communities they come from. They further cite that more research should to be undertaken to reveal the hidden costs of criminal policies as a social determinant of health. The Home Office (2006) highlight how significant data gaps prevent the building of a greater picture relating to young black people's overrepresentation in the criminal justice system. Mauer (1999) similarly points out that racial disparities in the criminal justice system should be a cause for alarm on both the strategic and policy level and that it requires a national conversation on the role of the racialization of crime and punishment. Alexander (2010) also reveals an ugly truth, namely that more black men are under correctional control than were enslaved in 1850. Maruna (2010) argues that the community must be involved in reintegrating prisoners back into the community that act as a form of 'justice ritual'. Justice rituals, he further argues, are meant to reaffirm and strengthen the wider moral order. It is right, therefore, to assume that by privileging the voices of men's experiences of both re-entry and journey towards desistance, there is a unique opportunity to expand these understandings in areas of policy research that are scant, under researched and under theorized. Maruna (2010) argues too that the reintegration of prisoners back into the community requires 'well-orchestrated rituals', but feels that ex-prisoner reintegration, as it is currently practised, is one such failing ritual that should be re-examined. Maruna's comments expose one of the overriding problems facing many black offenders, namely that the rituals associated with re-entry are empty, based on a series of systemic ritualized failures (structure) that restricts the returning 'former' offender's agency.

Stories abound

The stories black offenders tell of their experiences of criminal activity and engagement with the wider criminal justice system should enable them to narrate, to interpret, and to reinvent one's self by bringing coherence to one's life stories (McAdams, 1988). The challenge for navigating a racially stratified criminal justice system for black offenders is problematic if the processes and approaches taken to engage with their experiences compound the latent pathologies they face. On concluding a prison sentence, a former offender will be released, re-enter the community, and then hopefully be ready for a life free from crime, to ultimately desist. To do so, a former prisoner must be equipped with the necessary tools to reintegrate back into the community and contribute to its overall development by being reformed as a consequence of experiencing positive rehabilitative processes. However, little is known about what happens within the first few weeks of release. Petersilia (2001) argues that virtually no systematic, comprehensive attention has been paid by policy makers to deal with black people after they are released. It is my view that the lens, methodology, and modes of analysis regarding the journey taken by black offenders needs to be completely revised or, at least, that the support should be enlisted of the complimentary approaches to investigating the gaps in knowledge, flaws in framing, and associated problematics, where race and the racialization of crime is concerned. It is to this end I would like to turn to the development of a more participatory social science that operates less from the standpoint of the academic expert, but one that uses a co-produced and emancipatory approach.

Participatory social science

Denzin (2010) argues for a civic, participatory social science, a critical ethnography that moves back and forth beyond biography, history, and politics. This would involve the critical ethnographer producing texts that are grounded and co-constructed in both the political and personal worlds of everyday life. Doing this, in my view, would generate a counter-narrative designed to challenge notions of racialized subordination for black offenders, alongside producing new ways of seeing and responding to the complexities associated with racial reform within criminal justice and criminology as a discipline. There is a need to explore socially constructed racialized positions designed to provide a wealth of material for analysing how racism operates in the lives of black offenders in relation to broadening our understanding of how individual experiences link to, and reproduce, broader social patterns of inequality. Glynn (2014) argues that without any access to the lived experiences of black offenders, we will too easily formulate solutions that are out of sync with the realities of their lives and that would be ineffective or outright destructive. Without hearing their stories, we lose sight of those who hold real hope for the future, whose visions for community embrace peace and nonviolence. This is why hearing their stories told through their own words are important. Before black offenders are willing to terminate their offending behaviour they must begin to perceive what they are doing is unsatisfying, thus weakening their commitment to the sustainability of criminal activity. In essence, black offenders seeking to break from crime must fashion a new identity and develop a more 'pro-social' life. Hill-Collins (2000) argues that strengthening notions of self-definition as a way of challenging and eradicating stereotypical assumptions is an important consideration for black offenders who want to improve their lives. hooks (1991) likewise sees the understanding of black offenders' stories as a position and place of resistance that need to be navigated if black men are to liberate themselves from an oppressed social position. Therefore, any future research regarding black offenders should provide opportunities not just for self-reflection but scope for transforming into a new 'constructed self'.

Culturally sensitive research methods

Denzin (2003) further argues that the use of culturally sensitive research methods and approaches could succeed in creating space where black offenders will be able to hear their own stories, and the stories of others, free from judgement. Privileging the voices of black offenders this way would then create new and reframed life events that have meaning and significance rooted within a symbolic, metaphoric, and allegorical context. The occupation of a different personal space could be best articulated using 'performance' as the conduit. By doing so, creative representations of black offenders understandings of the racialization of crime and criminal justice systems may bring their insights and understandings to a more heightened prominence. Denzin (2010) suggests that, 'at the beginning of a new century it is necessary to re-engage the promise of qualitative research as a form of radical democratic process. We know the world only through our representations of it' (2010: 6). He concludes by arguing that performative social science paradigms may provide some new answers to old problems – in this case improving the life chances for black offenders who are struggling to reintegrate into a community where opportunities are blocked and they are denied access to the social structure that subordinates them. The histories of slavery, lynching, colonialism, race riots, the rise of the far right, and numerous issues past and present where crime has been racialized would suggest that the current race and crime project is far from complete.

To the now ...

Audre Lorde was an American writer, feminist, womanist, librarian, and civil rights activist, who dedicated both her life and her creative talent to confronting and addressing injustices of intersectional oppression. Her words encapsulate the deeper political aspirations for my book, grounding it within a wider black political continuum, where the racialization of crime and criminal justice is situated. More importantly, Lorde was known not just for her activism but for creative engagement with politics; she did not put a wedge between them. In her prophetic words lay a powerful existential position from which to begin the journey of my book. To Lorde politics and art were inextricably linked. She states: 'There are no new ideas, just new ways of giving those ideas we cherish breath and power in our own living' (1984: 129). Important here is the recognition that the proposition that is laid before you is building on what has gone before. Here Lorde guides my thinking regarding the past with a reassuring statement of intent: 'Through examining the combination of our triumphs and errors, we can examine the dangers of an incomplete vision. Not to condemn that vision but to later it, construct templates for possible futures, and focus our rage for change upon our enemies rather than upon each other' (1984: 130). A key connector to the sociological, criminological and black criminological imaginations is the location and importance of history, clearly expressed by Lorde:

> If history has taught us anything, it is for action for change directed against the external conditions of our oppressions is not enough. And we must fight that inserted piece of self destruction threat lives and flourishes like a poison inside of us, unexamined until it makes us turn upon ourselves in each other. (1984: 137)

As I join the cadre of those who, like Lorde, want change, it is important her words become embedded in our psyche, laying the foundation for the struggle towards a new future, so beautifully put by Lorde herself: 'We are making the future as we as bonding to survive the enormous pressures of the present and that is what it means to be part of history' (1984: 139). To be part of history is to know we have been here, that we have made a contribution, and, more importantly, connects us all to the shaping of a better world. This humble offering has been 40 years in the making, letting the artist in this criminologist speak with clarity. I am further hoping that all readers of my book will debate, discuss, and share their experiences of its contents, not as a definitive guide to the issues that are far too complex, messy, and long term, to do so, but to lay a foundation for more work, directions, and solutions to be undertaken. It is to this end I turn my attention for a move towards the development of a 'black arts infused critical race criminology'.

Reimagining Black Art and Criminology is an invitation to disrupt the sterility of current debates and discussions focussed on the lived experiences of black people who have come into contact with the criminal justice system, that still excludes perspectives and positions coming from progressive black scholars.

Organization of the book

Chapter 1: Reimagining a Black Art Infused Criminology

This chapter aims to reinvigorate the discussion about viewing black criminality through the lens of black art. Young's (2011) notion of a 'criminological imagination' informs important contemporary debates on crime. However, there is a distinct absence of a racialized context. Garner (2009) argues that the concept of racialization is based on the idea that the object of study should not be race itself, but the process by which race becomes meaningful in a particular context.

Chapter 2: The People Speak: The Importance of Black Arts Movements

This chapter explores the unique vantage point that black arts movements present when exploring the racialization of crime and criminal justice systems. Black arts movements, through activism and art, created new cultural institutions and conveyed messages of black pride, while at the same time reflecting on the impact of racism on black people's expressed art and literature.

Chapter 3: Shadow People: Black Crime Fiction as Counter-Narrative

Using black crime fiction, this chapter offers an interesting proposition when exploring black criminality. Namely, are the roles of the ethnographer and crime fiction writer interchangeable?

Chapter 4: Staging the Truth: Black Theatre and the Politics of Black Criminality

Although black theatre was, and still is, a powerful force within the wider theatrical landscape, this chapter focuses on the use of 'applied theatre' with black offenders.

Chapter 5: Beyond The Wire*: The Racialization of Crime in Film and TV*

The chapter looks at the representation of black criminality viewed through a film and TV lens. In spite of the success of TV shows like HBO's *The Wire*, black criminality and victimhood in contemporary film and TV tend to lean heavily on stereotypical and pathologized portrayals of black participation in crime.

Chapter 6: Strange Fruit: Black Music (Re)presenting the Race and Crime

This chapter examines the role of black music in relation to the study of the racialization of crime and criminal justice systems. Black music reveals key messages, insights, understandings, and perspectives that illuminate the connection to, and relationship with, the structural elements that have disproportionately criminalized, incarcerated, and executed many black people.

Chapter 7: Of Mules and Men: Oral Storytelling and the Racialization of Crime

This chapter explores the tradition of black storytelling and its possible role when reflecting on the impacts of racialization of crime and criminal justice on black offenders.

Chapter 8: Seeing the Story: Visual Art and the Racialization of Crime

This chapter posits that black visual art historically has provided an embodied space that moves beyond mere words, musical notes, and physical movement, demanding the observer stands still.. An interrogation of black visual art in relation to the racialization of crime and criminal justice could play an important rehabilitative function for black offenders.

Chapter 9: Speaking Data and Telling Stories

This chapter envisions a way for research data to be seen, heard, and experienced using a frame of reference that is unapologetically black, creative, and accessible to the wider community. The importance of breaking free from the peer review journal and conference circuit within academia requires the creation and production of criminological counter-narratives contesting some of the biased claims made by many white academics and scholars when disseminating research data centring on black criminality.

Chapter 10: Locating the Researcher: (Auto)-Ethnography, Race, and the Researcher

This chapter looks at researcher reflexivity as a disruptive and embodied practice, imbued with subjective, epistemological, and ontological concerns regarding how racialized knowledge is constructed and produced.

Chapter 11: Towards a Black Arts Infused Criminology

This chapter calls for a black art infused criminology that may provide a new platform to bring to the fore the black contribution to criminology, which is currently rendered invisible.

Provocations

At the end of each chapter I have written a provocation designed to incentivize you to question and probe further, in the hope it will spark you into action regarding further reading, research, curriculum development, or decolonizing work within your own research, pedagogy, or learning.

Dr Martin Glynn
May 2021

Beyond the Wall

*Written for the Resurrection Support Group
(Green Haven State Penitentiary, 1999)*

Precious moments like this
Are all we have to bind us
To each other
Empty memories
Filled with new thoughts
As we smile together
For the first time
Like innocent children
Learnin' a new game
Fragments of a broken past
Pieced together
To heal our pain
Which we reveal thru'
Glazed eyes 'N' silent tears
We become men
Brothaz and Sistaz on the same journey
Who have trod the different paths
But today we see the same things
Dream the same dreams
'N' escape into a secret world of
Laughter 'N' celebration
Thru' the darkness comes light
Thru' the light we step together
Holdin' on to the time we have left
Then the flow is broken
We embrace ... you leave
'N' I shed a tear
As the remnants of those moments
Evaporate like steam
I stand outside the prison walls look back 'N' say,
'Look beyond the wall brothaz 'N' sistaz
Look beyond the wall ...'

Reimagining a Black Art Infused Criminology

Chapter summary

This chapter calls for a discussion about black criminality viewed thorough a lens of black art. Racial disparities within the criminal justice system are widespread and their perpetuation weakens the collective cooperation in arresting the problems. The continuing existence of racial disparities within the criminal justice system in my view requires a counter-narrative response designed to invigorate new responses to old problems. The Sentencing Project (2008) argue that racial disparity in the criminal justice system operates when the proportion of a racial group within the control of the systems and structures is greater than the proportion of such groups within the general population.

Systemic change

The Ministry of Justice (2020) acknowledge there remains an over-representation of ethnic minorities within the criminal justice system and disparities in aspects of their treatment. The Lammy Review (2017) reflected an indictment on the criminal justice system as experienced by black people. It is clear that the case to address these disparities remains compelling. Lorde (1984) expresses the view that the 'master's tools will never dismantle the master's house'. It is, therefore, incumbent on any scholar who decides to challenge the orthodoxy to do so from a position that does not negate black epistemological concerns. Marable (2001) argues that, historically, it is black scholars who have theorized from the black experience who have often proposed practical steps for the empowerment of black people. In other words, there is a practical step between their scholarship and the struggle for racial parity, between social analysis and social transformation. The purpose of black scholarship, as Marable suggests, is more than restoration of identity and self-esteem; it is to use history and culture as tools through which black people interpret their collective experience for the purpose of transforming their actual conditions and the totality of the society all around them. Hall (1993) similarly sees black culture as a contradictory space that can never be simplified or explained in terms of binary opposites or statistical breakdowns. He goes further by suggesting that 'it is only through the way in which we represent and imagine ourselves that we come to know how we are constituted and who we are' (1993: 111).

Imaginations

Mills' (1959) notion of a 'sociological imagination' examines the ability to examine how society interacts and influences our lives, giving a rationale behind our actions. Also, Mills assists us making sense of our world and our place in it and talks of a sociological imagination that enables us to grasp both 'history' and 'biography' while engaging with the relation between the two. Important here is to ask a critical question about where the history of racialized oppression is situated within Mills' vision. Mills further states: 'Men are free to make history, but some men are freer than other. Such freedom requires access to the means of decisions and of power by which history may now be made' (1959: 226). As black people historically have had limited access to power, how realistic is the possibility of a radical reforming of the criminal justice system if the histories of racialized oppression places white privilege over black liberation. Young's (2011) notion of a 'criminological imagination' is, therefore, problematic when engaging in contemporary debates on the formations of crime, criminal justice, and criminology, where there is a distinct absence of a racialized context. This, in my view, exposes a gap to be filled. Garner (2009) argues that the concept of 'racialization' is based on the idea that the object of critical inquiry should not be 'race' itself, but the process by which race becomes meaningful in a particular context. It is my contention that, without the inclusion of a wider cadre of ideas coming from diverse scholars, criminology as a discipline is incomplete. Here, Young, when unpacking his 'criminological imagination', envisions a new future:

> Human beings are storytelling animals, they create stories of themselves and others. They devise narratives about themselves, they talk to their peers about these narratives, they tell stories to other people as exemplars, subcultures are a bundle narratives within which the social world hums, subcultures talking about themselves and subcultures talking about subculture. (2001: 89)

Again, admirable as Young's statement might be, there is clearly a problem when some sections of society are silenced and muted.

The black criminological imagination

Having grown weary and tired of the circular arguments associated within the discipline of criminology surrounding anything concerning the black presence, race, and racialization, in relation to crime and criminal justice, I decided to locate and position my book using a lens rooted in notions of a 'black criminology'. Russell (2002) previously called for the development of a black criminology, while Phillips and Bowling (2003) strenuously argued for minority perspectives in criminology. Unnever et al (2019) have now crystallized those aforementioned developments extending this historical continuum with the publication of their seminal work, *Building a Black Criminology: Race, Theory, and Crime*, which, as the title suggests, has laid a new foundation for more critical dialogue that will better respond to this scholarly invisibility. Cuneen and Tauri (2016) also express the need for a move towards a more critical indigenous criminology. It is, therefore, equally as important to recognize and pay tribute to the ongoing contributions from criminologists, scholar-activists, social-racial justice advocates, and post-colonial scholars; across the world, who are part of a contemporary movement of ideas designed to make the discipline of criminology more accountable for its claims where race and non-white peoples are concerned. Fanon (1952) similarly set a tone for notions of a 'black criminological imagination' when he wrote:

> The white man is sealed in his whiteness
> The Black man in his blackness
> We shall seek to ascertain the directions of this dual narcissism
> And the motivations that inspire it. (1952: 3)

Fanon's notion of dual narcissism suggests that the weight of a racialized history requires a revision of the self-fulfilling narrative to one that is transformed through new emancipatory thinking defined in its own terms. Staples (1960) argues that a black criminology will reveal how crime is racialized and calls for the gulf between the black academic community and the black masses to be closed. Cruse (1967: 565) also urges us to move beyond popular debates regarding black scholarship and racial advancement and sets out a blueprint for black scholars to adhere to:

> [B]lack intellectuals must at all costs avoid slavish borrowing and uncritical importations of ideologies and strategies from other cultures. The Black experience is unique and the irrevocable imperative of the cultural self-demands to be treated as such. Those who cannot remember the past, are condemned to repeat it. (1967: 565)

Thornberry (1990) asserts that criminology's boundaries are fuzzy and calls for a revision, positioning it within a 'cultural literacy' paradigm. Cultural literacy sees that all knowledge is not equally valued. Barak (1991) too suggests that white male bias in criminal justice and criminology suppresses the socio-historical context for making sense of the 'black experience' in relation to crime and justice that, in turn, distorts the overall development of a wider global conversation on crime and justice as a whole. Siegal and Zalmon (1991) express the view that the criminal justice system sees traditional social science approaches that are not inclusive in terms of methodological rigour, thinking, and presentation. It is, therefore, important to push criminology to undergo change. I further contend that racialized insights into crime are not solely the domain of academics and is a shared space that extends to insights and understandings coming from the wider community. Liamputtong (2010) calls for researchers to undertake research that is both sensitive and responsible, placing marginalized groups at the centre of the process. The need, therefore, to undertake research that challenges biased assumptions and values in relation to criminology and its racialized contexts and constructs becomes a rallying cry for all criminologists who are tired of seeing the proliferation and growth of racial disparities in the wider criminal justice system. Barnes et al (2014) call for prophetic modes of inquiry and suggest we need to reframe the way Western scholarship is produced in the way claims on knowledge are made. Engaging with the experiences of the historically oppressed, alongside acknowledging the often troubling complexities inherent in undertaking such a mission reveals how race and crime should build on the foundations laid by historical movements designed to bring change for black peoples. This new work requires a black epistemology that provides a comprehensive analysis of the structural aspects of black criminality written by black academics, connected to the wider so-called mainstream agenda.

Black epistemological space

Phillips and Webster (2014) ask if the legacy of racism, stereotyping, black criminality, and policies that privileges whites over blacks has declined or decreased. Bell (1992) argues that black people should reform civil right strategies rooted in notions of 'racial realism', as opposed to 'racial idealism'. Racial idealism posits that all races are similar and can transcend dfferences and can get along with other. Racial realism on the other hand accepts that discrimination based on race is a cultural norm within society. Important here is how racial realism produces differential racialization. Gabbidon (2007) similarly argues that there is no singular theory that explains racial disparities in crime and justice, which suggest further development of these theoretical constructs is required. Gabbidon et al (2004) further argues that the black scholarly exclusion from the study of crime as a whole, including studies of race and crime is well documented. This position would suggest that black progressive black scholars must ground themselves within a racial realist paradigm, as opposed to a racial idealistic position, that sees colour blindness as the basis for its assumptions. Phillips et al (2020) likewise point out that rather than engaging with race, criminology has tended to focus on statistically driven explanations of race and disproportionality in the criminal justice justice rather than examine the qualitative complexities and contradictions. Emirbayer and Desmond (2012) sadly express the view that our understanding of the racial order will remain forever unsatisfactory so long as we fail to turn our analytic gaze back upon ourselves in relation to race and crime. The contemporary understandings of crime and punishment in modern society are dominated by issues such as 'mass incarceration', 'surveillance', 'cybercrime', and 'security studies', underpinned with some more minor constructs that generate, maintain, and sustain significant social divisions within the wider criminal justice system. Gilroy (2008) argues that the understanding of crime requires a detailed historical investigation that will raise further and more speculative questions about how we understand crime as a whole. Gilroy goes further and expresses the view that many white historians have failed to include or examine the historical context of black life within its overall analysis of crime and punishment as a whole.

Black criminology arrives

In March 2018 I was fortunate enough to be invited to a 'race and crime' symposium at the London School of Economics, where I met one of the most important and influential advocates of the need for a 'black criminology', Katheryn Russell-Brown. Katheryn coined the term 'black criminology' as far back as the 1990s, on account of the dissatisfaction at not seeing a coherent modus operandi for looking at black criminality and its formations. For Russell-Brown (2019) a black criminology:

- *needs* to adequately contextualize how blackness impacts criminal offending, victimization, and justice system processing;
- *offers* a more comprehensive understanding of how race works in the criminal justice system;
- *requires* an engagement with race and to discuss it as more than an independent variable in the research;
- *envisions* examining how race impacts the administration of justice.

Russell-Brown further argues that there is a wealth of research that analyses black involvement in the criminal justice system, but there needs to be an overarching framework from which to view these critiques. A black criminology, therefore, invites a (re)envisioning of so-called mainstream theories of crime and their interplay with 'race'. I would also like to add that the telling of the black criminological will also not be subservient to the dominance or the dictates of white criminologists who, in spite of their profile and positionality with so-called mainstream criminology, have not succeeded in bringing crime down, and certainly not reduced the impact of racialization on the lives of black people and the criminal justice system. Unnever et al (2019) argue that criminology as a discipline would be enriched by formerly adapting a black criminology that recognizes the racialized nature of black offending, details the racialized pathways to crime, illuminates how race is situated in relation to the wider criminal justice system, and advocates for race-centred approaches to prevention and rehabilitation. Agozino (2010) also asserts that criminology as a discipline must learn from history in order to advance the discipline itself, pointing to the histories of slavery and colonialism. Agozino further suggests that history cannot be disconnected from black people's overall engagement with, and connection to, their criminality. Chilisa (2012) also argues that the concerns and worldviews of colonized people should be understood through their own assumptions, concerns, and perspectives.

Chilisa feels that researchers and other related disciplines that aim to silence, marginalize, and alienate transformative perspectives within criminology must be part of a process of 'decolonization' within the discipline. I equally feel that a repositioning of debates on race and criminal justice are impotent without efforts to empower black scholars. In order to ground the call for an embedding of a black criminological imagination within mainstream criminology, much the same as its predecessors as mentioned earlier, I wanted to cite important contributions where such an imagination could be embraced.

What no theories?

The following list is a small roll call of specific theoretical perspectives that, in spite of being developed, seldom make their way onto the criminology top table, as well as providing a context for the utilization of a black art infused criminology:

- *Black criminology* assumes that white people constructed a racially stratified society and that the history of black people is not comparable to that of whites.
- *Post-colonial criminology* argues against conventional criminological assumptions. For black people, a history of subjugation – slavery, colonization, and apartheid – requires an analytical lens that focuses on the architects of politics and history that has been racialized.
- *Southern theory* focuses on how knowledge takes shape amid global power dynamics that are marked by authority, exclusion, and inclusion determined by colonialism. It emphasizes global inequalities between intellectuals and institutions, space and places in ways that discredit, subordinate, and ignore Aboriginal, indigenous and first nation scholars.
- *Cultural criminology* is a theoretical, methodological, and interventionist approach to understanding relations between social order and ideas about crime and its control, as creative constructs within processes of meaning making. It highlights and exposes how power affects the way rules are made and broken.
- *Narrative ciminology* highlights the ways that stories of crime influence crime and other harms. It is not a standpoint of appreciation for stories but instead frames its studies of offender stories and media narratives that shape various harm-doing policies.
- *Intersectionality* rests on the understanding that human beings are shaped by the interaction of their different social locations, which occur within a context of connected systems and structures of power

where such processes expose how multiple forms of privilege and oppression are created.

- *Critical race theory* has been widely associated with law, education, and, more recently sport, and uses storytelling as the basis of its theorizing as a means of privileging the voices of those who are oppressed and subordinated by white privilege and supremacy.

As criminology is expanding and growing, it is incumbent for both established and new scholars to recognize the need for new, improved, and more competent ways of framing the arguments surrounding race and the racialization of crime and the criminal justice system. On the day when the doctoral ethics committee adjudicated on my research proposal, I remember vividly how uncomfortable I felt at having to defend my literature review, when the consensus was that I should have reflected more diversity in my literature regarding the theoretical ideas I wanted to use within my research. Countering the committee's response, I inquired as to how many of those who sat before me included 'race' within their original doctoral proposals. The silence was deafening. I further pointed out that if a doctoral research project was predicated on a 'contribution to knowledge' then my justification was that much work – theoretical or otherwise – emerging from black scholars has been traditionally excluded. Therefore, my review of literature was an honest reflection of this omission. Important here is the recognition that non-white scholars have made a major contribution to the understandings of crime and its formations from many disciplines, countries, and periods of history. It is our job to (re)discover them and include them in any future dialogues and discussions we undertake.

Reflection

It would be very easy at this point to adopt a position of some of my white colleagues, who seek to present rhetorical posturing that tries to outdo each other, revealing some kind of moral authority over a discipline that has failed to provide adequate responses to why people who look like me – be they scholars, activists, practitioners, criminal, or victims – are still treated less favourably on account of racially deterministic rhetoric that passes off for credible thinking when it comes to framing the embodiment of blackness, politically, socially, and historically. It is, therefore, appropriate to begin this journey by unpacking the role of historical black arts movements. Important here is in the recognition that organized responses to oppression are nothing new, whether it is the Chartist movement, a working class movement that emerged in 1836 to gain political rights and influence for the working classes in the United Kingdom, through to the Black Lives Matter movement that emerged from the death of 17-year-old Trayvon Martin in 2012. Equally as important are the histories of human and civil right movements that have been seminal in the way black oppression was, and is, expressed where the artist/s have communicated messages of motivation, hope, rebellion, and disruption, bringing people together for the purpose of change. Without those movements, much of what I will be exploring in the book will have no foundation and could get lost in translation. As stated previously, this book does not lay claim to a new theory. It is merely a platform to lay the foundation for a new generation of scholars who will seek to engage with the content, hopefully spurring those committed to change to develop a 'black arts infused black criminological imagination' to contest the dominant narrative that has all too often air-brushed out many black contributions to the so-called mainstream criminology canvas. Historically, black arts movements, through a combination of activism and art, generated cultural institutions, conveyed messages of black resistance, resilience, and pride, while at the same time reflecting on the damaging effects of systemic racism. While many of these movements were short-lived, their work has had a lasting influence on me and my work. Important here is the unique vantage point that black arts movements represent when exploring the racialization of crime. The 'godfather' of the 1960s US black arts movement, Amiri Baraka (aka Leroi Jones) (1963) argues that black people were enslaved as Africans, lost their heritage through racist oppression, and have had to adapt ever since. Art therefore became the life blood, that was an expression of dreams, desires, and the challenges associated with the pursuit of freedom and justice. In essence, Baraka was alluding to an important facet of black life, namely that art for black people attached itself to the dismantling of those structures that perpetuated any notions of white supremacy and racialized oppression.

Let the journey begin.

Provocation

Does Young's (2011) 'criminological imagination' enhance or hinder the need for a black arts infused criminology?

2

The People Speak: The Importance of Black Arts Movements

Chapter summary

This chapter examines the importance of studying historical black arts movements alongside evaluating my involvement in the radical black arts movement in the United Kingdom during the 1980s. My need to further explore black arts movements has given me a new impetus into how these valuable creative insights can be used as a pedagogic tool when exploring the criminal justice system as a whole.

The need for a black aesthetic

Defranz and Gonzalez (2014) argue that theoretically driven black performativity helps us decipher the imperatives of blackness. Blackness in this context is developing a unity of experience/s rooted in the social–historical–political–cultural aspects of not being white. Lynn (2005) further asserts that scholars with interests in 'race and culture' should develop new ways at looking at the links between race, culture, and pedagogy. Therefore, black arts movements become a key driver when examining the pragmatics associated with black arts and the criminological imagination. Pragmatics studies the ways in which context contributes to meaning, and encompasses theory, conversation, approaches to language behaviour, sociology, linguistics, and anthropology. Crawford (2017) similarly sees black arts movements as taking a position that is unapologetically black, and sees the artist/s as the shaper of notions of blackness, that are ongoing and constant, that require constant reworking and revising. Counsell and Wolf (2001) see black cultural identity as the foundation of social organization reproducing and reinforcing patterns of inequality connected with structures of social power – criminal justice being one such structure. It could be argued that it is 'counter-narratives' that through art expresses the way in which black identities are suppressed; the mobilization of a movement can then stand to assist racial parity within society, as will be discussed in this chapter. Baraka (2011) sees black people as oppressed, with the right of self-determination, expressed through art, acting as a conduit from which to speak without restriction. This remains the valid issue where black people (offenders included) can express themselves through institutions of their own creation. Baraka goes on to state:

> [T]hat is the continuing task we face, as revolutionary black artists and intellectuals, to make cultural revolution. To fight in the superstructure, in the realm of ideas, philosophies, the arts, academia, the class struggle between oppressed and oppressor. To re-create and maintain our voice as a truly self-conscious, self-determining entity, to interpret and focus our whole lives and history. And create those organizations and institutions that will finally educate, employ, entertain, and liberate us! (2011: 31)

Baraka, one of the architects of the radical US Black Arts Movement (BAM), understands that, for black people, art is not just a spectacle to observe or be entertained by, but is a driver of political and social change. Neal (1968) saw the BAM in the 1960s as a place of resistance that was opposed to any concept of the artist being alienated from the community from which they came. This movement, Neal further expressed, was the aesthetic and spiritual sister of the black power movement. As such, it envisioned art that spoke directly to the needs and aspirations of black people. Neal concluded by positing that the black arts movement proposes a radical reordering of the Western cultural aesthetic as a desire for self-determination and nationhood. Neal's position acknowledged that black intellectuals of previous decades failed to ask critical question of white society and, in doing so, created the impetus for black artists to 'speak truth to both power and history'. Like Neal, I feel that the black artist must address themselves to this reality in the strongest terms possible and play a meaningful role in the transformation of society. An example in practice was that of Hoyt William Fuller, who pursued and established himself at the highest level in journalism but became frustrated with the disconnect between glossy magazines promoting bourgeois ideas regarding the struggle for black freedom. In 1961, he became editor of the *Negro Digest*, which became an important platform for many black arts movement writers, and devoted his life to black culture and arts. Harrison (2014) similarly recognized that the (re)branding of black theatre required an exploration of black theatrical performances beyond popular culture. In essence, a theatre that was bold, political, and unapologetically black. Such expressive products, as Harrison sees it, did not diminish the breadth of black performativity, but instead locates black theatre clearly in a space where struggle, validity, and embodiment gave voice not just to black aspiration but to black oppression – hence the importance of black arts movements, which historically have continued to disrupt white expectations of what black creativity can or cannot do.

Ongoing struggle

Alexander (2010) points out that racism has merely been redesigned not alleviated. Art, therefore, shines a light of cover up and deceit, to expose hidden truths, expressed by artists. How then can arts practices become embedded in criminal justice systems where 'punishment' trumps 'rehabilitation', and the ensuing retributive culture fails to ameliorate racial disparities within the wider criminal justice system? If racism, as Alexander points out, has been redesigned, where will the new stories about racial injustice within the criminal justice system come from? How will art begin a new chronicle for the next generation of artists and activist scholars to use as a spearhead for information, transformation, and change? The need to reveal those forgotten and invisible voices who, despite their crimes, come from the same cultural, political, and social bond as me, is ever present and ongoing. It is to my own personal relationship to black arts movements that I would like to turn to now. I became involved with prison work in the early 1980s. Even though I had come from a background of activism, I was told by a dear African-American friend and committed activist, Linda Thurston, while working in Boston (US) in 1985, that if I wanted to do real activist work with black people I needed to start with prisons, because that's where many of us were. Initially I started writing to black prisoners and accidently drifted into setting up arts-based residencies in prisons, 50 in total, between 1993 and 2015. The turning point came back in the mid-1980s when I was asked to run a residency with a group of volatile black offenders in Long Lartin maximum security prison, based in the United Kingdom. I was brought into the prison to engage the men around issues such as black history and politics, where the outcomes would be translated into creative practices. At that time incarcerated, the black men I worked with expressed having a sense of reconnection to themselves as men, where their lived experiences outside of their engagement with the criminal justice system were given voice. For those who could not read or write, the arts became a vehicle for them to explore who they were, what their purpose in life was, alongside reaffirming, and restoring, notions of manhood, which was always central to my work then, and now.

Milestone

The next milestone came when my dear friend, the late Anne Peaker, suggested I use the Unit for Arts and Offenders (now the Arts Alliance) to articulate the voice of black offenders based on the neglect of black offenders' cultural needs. In consultation with Anne, it was suggested that we work towards building a project around the identified needs and, through research, hopefully bring some change. After a seminar held in 1995, at the university of Leicester, called 'The Arts in a Multi-Cultural Society', I delivered a presentation arguing for the need to expand the arts for black people in the community, into prisons. Both Anne and her close colleague Jill Vincent decided to create a study that specifically focused on black offenders and the arts. The key objective was to present important insights that would inform future policy making regarding black offenders and the rehabilitative processes that impacted on their lives. Emerging out of this event a proposal was developed and, amazingly, resourced. I proceeded to work alongside a group of talented black artists, male and female, drawn from all different arts backgrounds, all in conjunction with the Unit for Arts and Offenders, who drove the research. In consultation with Anne, we decided to call the project 'Nuff Respect: the creative and rehabilitative needs of black offenders'. However, in spite of its overwhelming success the project has never continued beyond its initial delivery. Unfortunately the scope of this book does not give me space to unpack the detail of the project. However, based on one on the key recommendations, it did give me the basis of an approach to working with black offenders that is with me to this day:

> [B]lack led creative arts projects should be provided, through which black prisoners (specifically) may be helped to develop a better informed and more positive sense of

their own identity. Such projects might include discussion, debate, critical analysis as well as cultural determined work around rites of passage, as part of existing programmes on assertiveness, anger management, and parenting, with recognition that Eurocentric practices in this area are not always suitable for men with different cultural/racial backgrounds. (Peaker, 1998: Recommendation 6.1.5)

Over a period of many years I have delivered many projects specifically targeted at black male offenders. My workshop approach at that time would typically involve group bonding and teaching from a point of the men's prior knowledge. I adapted my approach in each situation to maximize the possibilities for growth and change. At that time I did not have a coherent methodology, evaluation strategy, or academic context to what I was doing. In order to create a safe space, I needed to be able to build credibility by using culturally relevant approaches. My methods were mostly underpinned by the cultural understandings that were familiar to the men. Over time I developed a range of projects; fatherhood, masculinity, rites of passage, black history, politics, and literature, using performance as the driver. As word spread, I was offered more residencies. I felt I had 'arrived', especially when the African-American community heard about what I was doing and invited me to the US. In 1999, I undertook a creative residency in Green Haven State Penitentiary, in upstate New York, working alongside Dr Garry Mendez, the founder and director of the National Trust for the Development of African-American Men. The residency focussed on my strengthening the men's black self-concept, using art to rework their own personal narrative outside their negative social labelling. In the evaluation, it was expressed that the men felt humanized by the experience. I knew I was onto something, as I now had an international reputation.

Arising conflict

On my return, I decided that arts-driven work that combined black politics and culture was the way to go. However, many prisons were cynical and intimated by the change in black men's shift in self-concept and identity, which resulted in many attempts to sabotage my work. In doing so, several prisons pushed my work from being 'pro-black' to more 'culturally inclusive' spaces. This ultimately led to conflict among black and white prisoners, who at times did not have the coping skills when sharing space with individuals with whom they had racial conflict on the wings. This was when I began to connect my readings about the importance of movements. I was a lone individual and was weakened by operating in a solitary capacity. Throughout the 1990s I continued to mobilize black prisoners through dialogue groups to engage with prison regimes to raise matters of concern. This was an early indicator that incarcerated men were not only capable of organizing themselves, but were skilled in making demands on prison regimes with significant gains. It was at that time I really began to understand the relationship between agency and structure and that art-driven rehabilitative work created a perfect intersection from which to operate. I further asked of myself, 'What do prisons do for black prisoners?'

Awakening

Studying black arts movements was the key driver in politicizing myself, that in turn would enable me to transcend the clutter of racist impositions about how I defined my sense of self and what I did. Investigating these movements improved my self-concept and decolonized my thoughts on so many levels. It was in the knowledge that black arts movements resisted traditional Western influences and found new ways to present the black experience that greatly appealed to me. On several occasions I witnessed the expressions of outrage and anger when those incarcerated individuals I worked with realized that the black contribution to the world had been rendered invisible and was hidden from them. It was precisely why so many black arts movements sprang up in the first place. Slavery and colonialism, in particular, were both predicated on exploitation of land, destruction of civilizations, and control over generations of black people. Important here is in understanding the socio-political function of black art. As a lecturer of both black history and black studies, the emotional and psychological impact on black offenders has never ceased to amaze me, when they discovered the richness of their past heritage that they have been denied. Black art in this context became, and still does become, a way of creating an immersive and embodied space, much the same as Boal's (2000) 'legislative theatre', which involved prisoners themselves using artistic expression to actualize 'praxis' within criminal justice settings such as prison. Like Boal, I saw myself as part of a wider continuum seeking validation for those who have violated society's rules, who in doing so have been treated less humanely, based not merely on their crimes but the colour of their skin.

Winston Churchill Fellowship

In 2014, I was awarded a Winston Churchill Fellowship, the key aim of which was to look at models of good practice where addressing fatherlessness, father hunger, and father deficit among young men has created stronger communities, in the US city of Baltimore. The results of my Baltimore residency landed me the prestigious Pol-Roger award for 'outstanding contribution to society and the citizen', and I concluded the following:

> Being in Baltimore has enabled me to view crime in a whole different way. I have become and am now seen as a public intellectual, inasmuch as I occupy two spaces equally but different; community and academia. It feels like waking up in a strange room and things have changed. Many things have changed, not least me. The irony of feeling both liberated and trapped at the same time is a strange feeling, but one that I'm trying to manage. I can't go back to what I was and I am not yet fully formed in terms of being re-birthed as a criminologist. I have felt at times disconnected and dislocated, and wandered around in a liminal space waiting to make some kind of transition into something. Like many academics I occasionally hover like a humming bird and at times being frightened to confront things that you have to let go of. In reality I am meeting new people, having new experiences, and have acquired fresh perspectives, not just about crime, but people. In conversation with a good friend he made a comment about notions of invisibility and referred to this state of being as like a 12th man (Substitute) on a cricket team. I reflected on my own situation and realize how at times I feel like the 12th man. I was told that any new journey would be lonely, transforming, and at times uncomfortable. The desire to be a team player, but being relegated to the bench because your style of play doesn't suit people is very painful. Flair, individuality, and operating outside the box, are all qualities that scares a team that have been playing the same formation and tactics for the longest while. I do not want to be invisible, but if I continue to settle for second best, compromise myself, or play into other people's mindset, and then I am destined to sit on the subs bench. I keep coming back to Ellison's prophetic speech. Why do I feel

this way? Maybe I'm invisible to me and need to become more visible. I smile and am grateful for Baltimore's invisible citizens letting me into their lives. I know why I'm here. More importantly I know who I am. (2010)

I thought I had arrived at a new place, full of optimism for change. I got my doctorate, landed a book deal, and built an international reputation for my work. But I was still no closer to realizing my ambition to see black arts embedded within criminal justice, in spite of the success I had in this area. In investigating matters further, I realized that there was a historical pattern of exclusion that was synonymous with air-brushing out the black contributions within the arts and sciences. I was painfully aware I was not alone, unique, or justified in feeling sorry for myself. The more I delved into this situation, the more I knew it was incumbent of me to continue the legacy by detailing its existence for the next generation following. In doing so, the continuity would be ongoing and kept alive.

The roll call

This section details some of the key movements that have assisted in shaping my consciousness and approach to working with black offenders. The onus is on those of us who know the past, to adapt, reshape, and reposition the outcome in new situations and contexts. For those of you reading this whose passions will be awakened, I urge you to conduct further research and delve into the detailed histories that lie before you. The following section is merely a route map to further study. This list is by no means exhaustive, but will whet your appetite.

Harlem Renaissance

The Harlem Renaissance was an intellectual, social, and artistic explosion centered in Harlem, New York City, spanning the 1920s, where racial pride was expressed through the production of literature, art, and music. The Harlem Renaissance served to uplift the African-American community. The movement embraced a wide variety of cultural perspectives and styles, including black politics, experimental forms in literature, theatre, visual art, dance, and music. Some common themes represented during the Harlem Renaissance were the impacts of slavery on emerging black identities, the effects of institutional racism, and how to convey the experience of modern African-American life. However, contemporary scholars such as me see the Harlem

Renaissance as much more than a literary or artistic movement, as it possessed a sociological–criminological element brought about by a new racial consciousness. Many critics have argued that the movement itself at times was too broad in orientation, while at the same time more radical African-American artists clashed with conservatives in the black intelligentsia, who took issue with elements of depictions of black life as serving mainly the white elites at that time.

The Niagara Movement

The Niagara Movement was founded in 1905 by a group of civil rights activists led by W.E.B. Dubois and William Monroe Trotter. The movement opposed racial segregation and the accommodation and conciliation of ideas promoted by African-American leaders such as Booker T. Washington, who believed the focus should be centred on education and work, to raise the aspirations and attainment of black people. The Niagara Movement responded to the injustices of the criminal justice system by challenging and contesting the courts and systemic oppression. Although the movement was short lived, by studying the Niagara Movement I gained an understanding of the importance of organizing around the mitigating factors that can defeat and thwart attempts to achieve social and racial justice. Another important factor in the movement was how intellectuals actively engaged and immersed themselves in the push towards social justice. Again, both Harlem Renaissance and the Niagara Movement laid powerful foundations from which future black movements were built. However, much of the Niagara Movement's ideas have been hidden and obscured from the wider public gaze, and are confined to the history books.

Négritude

Négritude was developed mainly by francophone intellectuals, writers, and politicians of the African diaspora during the 1930s, aimed at raising and cultivating 'black consciousness' across Africa and its diaspora. Négritude was founded by Martinican poet Aimé Césaire, Léopold Sédar Senghor (the first President of Senegal), and Léon Damas of French Guiana. Négritude intellectuals disavowed colonialism, and argued for the importance of a pan-African sense of being among people of African descent worldwide. The importance of the Négritude movement is that the focus of attention was rooted within a pan-European context, moving the lens from the US into a wider diasporic perspective. As a young poet, I was very influenced by Négritude's contesting of the colonial past expressed not just through political writings, but poetry, theatre, and music. Here, I want to draw attention to the fact that, although the movements were spread out over time and geographical location, they were all united by the need to eliminate racial oppression.

Black Arts Movement (US)

The Black Arts Movement (BAM) was an African-American-led art movement, active during the 1960s and 1970s. The movement was triggered by the assassination of Malcolm X. Famously referred to by Larry Neal as the 'aesthetic and spiritual sister of Black Power', BAM applied these same political ideas to art and literature. BAM resisted traditional Western influences and found revolutionary ways to present the black experience unapologetically. The poet and playwright Amiri Baraka (formerly Leroi Jones) is widely recognized as the founder of BAM. Due to brutalities of slavery and the systemic racism of Jim Crow, the black contribution to the arts often went unrecognized. Similarly, during the civil rights era, many black activists and artists paid more and more attention to the political uses of art and would show the possibility of creating a new 'black aesthetic', responding to the changing political and cultural climate by the creation of politically engaged work that explored the black cultural and historical experiences. As a dramatist I was hugely inspired and influenced by BAM, on account of growing up in the United Kingdom, angry, with little direction, and knowing what had gone before was too meek and mild. Little did I know that I would become embedded in our own version years later.

Black Arts Movement (United Kingdom)

The movement was founded around the time of the First National Black Art Convention organized by the Black Art Group and held at Wolverhampton Polytechnic in 1992. Artists included Rasheed Araeen, David A. Bailey, Black Audio Film Collective, Sonia Boyce, Eddie Chambers, Shakka Dedi, Denzil Forrester, Lubaina Himid, Claudette Johnson, Remi Kapo, Eugene Palmer, Keith Piper, Donald Rodney, Mark Sealy, Marlene Smith, and Maud Sulter. A key feature of the group was to contest and challenge the British arts establishment that for so long had ignored the contributions of non-white peoples in the visual arts world. Little known and written about were all the other components that made the movement significantly larger in orientation. What did emerge from the initial impetus of this movement was the response of poets, dramatists, storytellers, dancers, and numerous others who, like our African American cousins, were experiencing racism and oppression on a large scale and being denied access. Equally as important was the role played by the Rastafarian movement, reggae sound systems, carnivals, and numerous other artistic institutions that were complimentary components that made the overall thrust of the movement truly diverse across the whole UK black community. I came to prominence during that time and would frequently be asked to perform my poetry in galleries, community venues, and prisons. Similar to the BAM in the US during the 1960s, the UK black arts movement redefined the way black identity was perceived by wider society, enabled black art to push back against the establishment, as well as generating materials that are part of an ongoing legacy of black culture. Again, like most movements, it was short lived, but it has been superseded by a proliferation of other artists and art forms who continue to this day to push boundaries and change the landscape of contemporary black Britain.

Combahee River Collective

The Combahee River Collective was a black feminist organization active in Boston from 1974 to 1980. The collective was instrumental in highlighting that both the white feminist movement and the civil rights movement were not addressing their particular needs as black woman and, in particular, lesbians. They are perhaps best known for developing the Combahee River Collective Statement, a key document in the history of contemporary black feminism. The author Barbara Smith and other delegates attended the first 1973 regional meeting of the National Black Feminist Organization in New York City that provided the groundwork for the Combahee River Collective. The name commemorated an action at the Combahee River planned and led by Harriet Tubman on 2 June 1863, in the Port Royal region of South Carolina. The action freed more than 750 slaves and is the only military campaign in American history planned and led by a woman. The Combahee River Collective Statement was involved in the process of defining and clarifying the politics of black women in coalition with other progressive organizations and movements. In 1977, the Combahee River Collective argued that they would struggle together with black men against racism, while also struggling with black men about sexism. Important here is in the recognition that central to the role of all these movements was wrestling the complexities of patriarchy, that still to this day disjoints many attempts to unify gendered constructions pertaining to black life. When one surveys the stereotypical way that black life is portrayed within the media it needs to be recognized that there has always been ongoing attempts to reconcile fractures between black men and women, as well as creating space for dialogue that will bring more unity in the face of the adversity of fighting racial injustice.

National Black Arts Alliance

The National Black Arts Alliance (NBAA) was formed in 1985 by a group of community artists attending the Sheldon Trust, who considered that black art was being marginalized in the United Kingdom by funders, art audiences, and politicians alike. The founder and driving force was an amazing artist–activist, Su Andi. Over the years Su positioned the NBAA where it had a platformed voice and was taken seriously. And then again, the rug was pulled from the funding because of changes within Arts Council policy, which curtailed much of its groundbreaking work. However, Su's steadfast commitment and sheer determination created a legacy that may not be as visible as it was, but for those of us who were around at the time have continued to push the NBAA agenda in new directions.

Apples and Snakes

Apples and Snakes was launched in 1982, and established itself as a key organization for performance poetry nationally. Ironically at that time Apples and Snakes, in spite of being run mainly by white people, really took seriously the need to give a platform to people like me who, in spite of being a prominent spoken word artist, needed to share what was happening in the spaces I occupied in the criminal justice system. In those days we were seen as the alternative performance circuit working alongside poets from other contexts and situations. Even though the set up in the 1980s was not that sophisticated, I managed to share my work and at times the work of those I was working with. In some respects Apples and Snakes became a link between the prisons I was working with and the wider community that was not privy to what I was doing. The audiences were always politically engaged and connected the work I was doing to the wider movement of bringing the spoken word to the masses.

New Beacon Books

New Beacon Books was a British publishing house, bookshop, and international book service that specialized in black British, Caribbean, African, and African-American and Asian literature. Founded in 1966 by John La Rose and Sarah White, it was the first Caribbean publishing house in England. New Beacon Books was widely recognized as having played an important role in the Caribbean Artists Movement and in black British culture more generally. New Beacon Books was named after the Trinidadian journal *The Beacon*, which was published between 1931 and 1932. In 1967, La Rose and White began to function as a specialist bookstore. As an emerging poet, I would frequent the shop and converse with the heavyweights of diverse literatures. In some respects the bookshop was the place, much the same as the British radical movement in the 19th century, where you studied how to organize and politicize issues using reading and writing coming from Africa, Asia, and the Caribbean. At that time I was introduced for the first time to the politics of 'class', where I engaged with those who had many differing political alliances, all working together for a common goal of unifying against racialized oppression.

Walter Rodney Bookshop

Walter Rodney Bookshop, formerly Bogle-L'Ouverture Publications, was a radical London-based publishing company founded by Guyanese activists and Eric and Jessica Huntley in 1969. It was named in honour of two outstanding liberation fighters in Caribbean history, Paul Bogle and Toussaint L'Ouverture. The company began operating during a period in the United Kingdom when books by black authors or written with a sympathetic view of black people's history and culture were rare in mainstream bookshops in the United Kingdom. The birth of Bogle-L'Ouverture Publications was a direct response to the 1968 banning from Jamaica of historian and scholar Walter Rodney, who was then teaching at the University of the West Indies in Mona and outside the lecture halls had been sharing his knowledge and exchanging ideas with the island's working people, prompting the government's censure. Jessica Huntley had the idea of an annual book fair, which was later developed and eventually implemented as the International Book Fair of Radical Black and Third World Books, held between 1982 and 1995. After Walter Rodney was assassinated in Guyana in 1980, the bookshop was renamed to honour him. Following changes in the publishing industry in the 1980s, when small independent publishers and booksellers faced often insurmountable competition from large multinational conglomerates, the bookshop was forced to close in 1990. Again, I remember frequenting their bookshop and learning the nature of how art and politics were intertwined. In 2019 I met Eric Huntley, who was then in his 70s, and who told me that without the internet and other related technologies much of what was left of the shop after it shut was lost.

Race Today Collective

Race Today was a monthly (later bimonthly) British political magazine. Launched in 1969 by the Institute of Race Relations, it was from 1973 published by the Race Today Collective, which included figures such as Darcus Howe, Farrukh Dhondy, and Linton Kwesi Johnson. The magazine was a leading organ of black politics in 1970s Britain, until publication ended in 1988. The Race Today Collective aimed for a political rather than scholarly approach, based on a combination of libertarian Marxism and radical anti-racism. A notable member of the Race Today Collective was Linton Kwesi Johnson, who joined the group in 1974. His first book of poems appeared the same year under the Race Today imprint, and he later served as the magazine's arts editor. Race Today Publications was also one of the organizers of the International Book Fair of Radical Black and Third World Books, together with New Beacon Books and Bogle-L'Ouverture Publications. The importance here is how the Race Today Collective used art not as a mere spectacle to observe the human condition, but in the fight against oppression.

This roll call merely highlights that black arts movement are an integral, not peripheral, component of the wider black struggle that cannot be divorced from the issues facing black people in relationship to their lived experiences in relation to the racialization of the criminal justice system. If culture is underpinned by collective meaning and identity, then an assessment of the cultural rehabilitation of black offenders is warranted here. Freire (1970) points out that the oppressed are better placed at times to understand their oppression, and argues their voices must speak and be heard. Denzin (2010) similarly points out that for 'subordinated and oppressed voices' to be heard, they must be assisted in their desire to 'transcend their silences'. Historically, within criminology, the voice of the victim is expressed through theoretical application, careful analysis, and drawing significant conclusions.

Reflection

It is my contention that any attempt to make objective assessments of black criminality, without taking into consideration the social, historical, and political components that shapes the trajectory or criminal activity, will be both flawed and incomplete in their claims. If we are to learn anything from these movements, it is not to root them in nostalgic reflection, but to critique and analyse their strengths and weaknesses, and to build on what they started. In doing so, not only will the continuity of development be extended, but we will be one step closer to emancipation for black people as a whole, where new contemporary black arts movements can play a major role in achieving this aim. A concluding point is to encourage readers of this book to investigate the wider role of art within liberation struggles worldwide. Black arts movements are merely a small representation of a wider continuum of art and its relationship to history, politics, and culture. The next part of this journey focuses on black crime fiction. In spite of its absence within so-called mainstream publishing, black crime fiction has served as an important source of entertainment for readers, as well as providing insights into the world of black criminality, one that attempts not just to solve crime but to depict the social conditions that inform how black criminality is produced.

Provocation

What role should black arts movements play in your own teaching and learning regarding race and the racialization of crime and criminal justice systems?

Shadow People: Black Crime Fiction as Counter-Narrative

Chapter summary

Within this chapter I explore how black crime fiction operates much the same as a researcher investigating the complexities of black life through immersive observation such as ethnography. Black crime fiction, I would argue, lifts the veil on black criminality, victimhood, and offending, much the same as any other crime fiction genre. However, additionally, what black crime fiction does, through character interaction, plot construction, propelled by a black vernacular, is to shine a light on the nuances of race, that shape elements of black criminality obscured by much of so-called mainstream criminology, which at times fails to capture, engage with, or represent black life, and its relationship with society and history.

Troubling thoughts

Out of all the chapters in this book, this one has proved to be the most challenging, mainly because of a lack of clarity. However, Ramdarshan (2019), when writing about the lack of representation of people of colour among children's book authors and illustrators, enabled me to reframe my focus:

> Take collective action to break down the systemic barriers to representation of creators of colour. We know that people of colour are under-represented in the creative and cultural sectors. In this report we argue that one of the challenges

to changing this is to confront a negative cycle of barriers which are reflective of those seen within our society more generally. (Ramdarshan, 2019: 15)

Similarly, I would argue that criminology, in its vision, should seek to provide for, and validate, new routes of access for stories of crime, be they fiction, or non-fiction, as a way of embedding and validating more diverse epistemological lenses from which to view the racialization of crime. Mordhorst (2008) argues for the reintroduction of experimental elements into academic approaches to criminological history. Mordhorst further argues that the story as counter-narrative method, may provide us with new insights into why some narratives attain hegemonic status, and how this can help us to understand the construction and function of historical consciousness. Colvin (2015) similarly sees the power of the dominant discourse is to include some stories as tellable and exclude others as marginal and abnormal. McGregor (2020) further argues that criminologists have written a rather sanitized, carefree history of the origins of their discipline. This discipline has much to hide, however, and criminologists' strict adherence to principles and claims of 'objectivity' and' neutrality' have helped hide the unspoken task that is criminology from view. There is a need to excavate the hidden history of criminology from the basement of scientific criminology. This excavation requires the use of tools sensitive to oppression and conflict, to recover, rewrite and explain the history of criminology. It could be argued that black crime fiction is available to writers and criminologists alike, based on not being included in the tapestry of journals, books, and other formats, that boxes into a corner creative approaches to criminological research and investigation. Therefore, black crime fiction obscures a deeper issue within criminology itself – namely, whose stories do we tell? In what form are those stories told? And who tells those stories?

Black crime fiction

Penzler (2009) argues that black crime fiction is very different in orientation from that produced by writers based on the socio-historical that informs the genre. Woods (1996) builds on Penzler's argument by expressing the view that the black presence in so-called mainstream crime fiction remains both hidden and obscured, based on the racialized exclusion that plagued many black writers trying to get their work out there. As discussed in previous chapters, the black arts movement did give a platform and space for black writers to flourish. Important here is to contextualize black crime fiction politically. With a history of racial subjugation that emerged from slavery, colonialism, civil–human rights movements, apartheid, etc, access to the means of producing and distribution within so-called mainstream outlets was not a real option or consideration for many black writers. What was very evident was that black mobilization around arts movements enabled the stories that were written to be shared with other black people. Woods cites a key period of growth for black novelists as the 1980s and 1990s, where there was a broadening of the black experience away from crime. This in effect means that black criminality within many contemporary black novels was part of the narrative depictions of black life, not the key driver. Writers such as Toni Morrison, Alice Walker, Terry McMillan, Charles Johnson, John Edgar Wideman, Gloria Naylor, and Ernest Gaines, alongside many others, moved the genre of black fiction into new and varied terrains, with a rich tapestry of characters reflecting the complex and diverse nature of black life being portrayed with raw openness, honesty, and sensitivity. However, standing out from the pack was Walter Mosley, who revised the hard-boiled detective novel fit for black readers, with his street-wise detective Easy Rawlins. Mosley's depiction of a black character who not only knew the streets, but the community in which he lived, transcended the traditional genre, where the white hardboiled detective was usually an isolated figure with little or no connection to the community in which he or she resided.

Redressing the balance

Here, Gifford (2013) reminds us to redress our understanding of black fiction by seeing the contribution of black writers as redrawing the boundaries of the genre. Russell-Brown (2019) cites the need for distinctive black criminology that focuses attention towards blackness as a central organizing theme in examining the way the criminal justice treats race as a starting point for criminological inquiry. Russell-Brown further invites a re-envisioning of mainstream theories of crime and their interplay with race. It is my view that black crime fiction can teach us more than academically written texts about black criminality, as the stories look at urban life from a perspective that reveals how black people really live and how their lives affect the world around them. However, there is still a paucity of black crime fiction writers in comparison to their white counterparts. Using a lens of black crime fiction may, therefore, offer an enterprising proposition from which explore Russell-Brown's goals within a black criminological framework, while at the same time seeing the important role that black crime fiction may play to widen our understanding of black criminality in its many guises.

Expansion

Historically, authors of black crime fiction have expanded the genre of crime fiction overall. While writers of classical crime fiction concentrated on solving the crimes and finding the criminal at the end of the novel, the writers of black crime fiction have heralded a significant change in the tone of this type of fiction. In traditional crime fiction the issue of racism usually resulted in a clash between white and black characters. In black crime fiction the (black) protagonist is aware of their blackness and knows what it means to be black in a society dominated by white people. This state of affairs makes black crime fiction more nuanced in orientation, as transcends 'race and racism' as the glue that can impede a more empowering lens from which to look at the black presence in crime fiction as a whole. Black crime fiction, with its focus on incarceration, urban street spaces, criminal exploits, and confrontation with white authority has also given birth to new sub-genres; hip-hop, ghetto, and urban fiction, have all now exploded onto the literary scene, and owe a lot of their contemporary positioning in the market place to their predecessors. As much as this position is to be welcomed, the cynic in me feels that this proliferation of these new genres are rooted in notions of 'interest convergence'. The term 'interest convergence' (Bell, 1995) indicates that change for black people only took place when the interests of white people were satisfied. Black crime fiction should be actively promoted by criminologists and other related scholars to keep the legacy of past works alive, as well as being used to explore the periods in which black criminality operated in the minds of crime fiction writers at particular periods of history.

Insider–outsider

Generally, 'insider researchers' are those who choose to study a group to which they belong, while 'outsider researchers' do not belong to the group under study. Bonner and Tolhurst (2002) outlined three key advantages of being an 'insider' in the research domain:

- a significant understanding of a group's culture;
- the ability to interact naturally with the group and its members;

• a previously established, and therefore greater, relational intimacy with the group.

The 'insider' positioning views the research process and products as co-constructions between the researcher and the participants in the research; it regards the research participants or respondents as active informants to the research; and attempts to give voice to the informants within the research domain (Denzin and Lincoln, 1999). As such, these perspectives allow the researcher to conduct research 'with' rather than 'on' their group. Glasgow (1980) further argues that the researchers investigating black life need at least some knowledge of black history, an awareness of the social and political conditions of black life, and considerable familiarity with ghetto dwellers, culture, and language. Glasgow further argues that researchers also need to acquire and understand the screened and coded messages within black vernacular. Important here is understanding that the limitations of the criminologist can be strengthened by a community's engagement and involvement with the formulation, undertaking, and dissemination of research inquiries that will have an impact on their lives. Rich (2009) argues when recounting the stories of young black men who had experienced trauma as a consequence of street violence that, without access to their voices, we could formulate solutions that are out of sync with the reality of their lives. Research should illuminate lived realities much the same as fiction. Denzin (2010) directs our attention to the need to transcend the confines of the 'ivory tower' for all those who believe in the interconnection between critical inquiry and social justice. Could it be that fiction writers can inform criminologists, or should criminologists assist fiction writers with deeper and more theoretical insights into crime and, more importantly, so-called mainstream criminology?

Access

Hare (1973) asks black scholars to release themselves from the sterile repetition of whiteness in academia by decolonizing the mind in the pursuit of new knowledge. Hare recounts how the isolation of the ivory tower requires black scholars to develop new norms, values, and institutional structures guided by black-led epistemological concerns. To undertake such a task Clark (1965) puts forward the proposition of the 'involved observer', which encapsulates operating much the same as a crime fiction writer undertaking research for a novel, short story, or play. Clark coined the term 'involved observer' when engaging with a discussion around the black ghetto, where he cites key tenets for black researchers when investigating black life. Black researchers, as Clark argues, must:

1. ... be part of what is being observed;
2. ... join the lives of the people and seek to understand them;
3. ... demand participation in the community's rituals and customs;
4. ... be a social scientist that cannot be completely objective in terms of race;
5. ... not be preoccupied with methodology innumerable articles in scientific journals devoted to escapist trivia.

It is my contention that residents of inner-city communities who are exposed to extreme levels of poverty, crime, and violence are both the 'experts' and 'knowers' of their lived experiences.

The code

There are times when the people I talk to are angry and exhibit the kind of distress that for many would be frightening. Unless there is a concrete understanding of the streets, black life, racialized constructs, combined with the artistic vernacular that drives it, then valuable insights will be lost. As much as so-called mainstream criminological research is predicated on well-planned, resourced, committee-approached, university-backed, theoretically driven, work, as an 'on the road' criminologist, I am both the observer and chronicler of the events taking place, which extends the scope of how we undertake this type of work, alluded to by Clark (1965). Undertaking any criminological research with those who live in the same community and share a common cultural–racial heritage can and does create its own pressure, as working on your objectivity is testing at the best of times. However, anyone engaged in researching their passion will experience that difficulty at times. It is the management and handling of the difficulties that count. Many of the subjects of my inquiries have a story to tell. Stories of pain, hurt, loss, and trauma push you on all levels to ensure you do not let your personal feelings get in the way. With traditional forms of qualitative research, the ethics of not 'going native' are clearly important, so as not to breach the boundaries between the researcher and the subjects of the inquiry. So, where does the black criminologist struggle and the black fiction writer reign supreme when portraying black criminality? Could the imposition of stifling the expression of blackness within academia be to blame?

Blackness and the criminologist

'Blackness', a short-hand for 'black consciousness', centres on the understanding of the history of black oppression and subordination, by acquiring the tools to transcend its impacts. By using tactics of colour-blindness, operating within white privilege, any notion of my 'blackness' is seen at times as lacking in objectivity. So, how does the expression of my blackness enhance or impede the possibility of academic validation, when one is constantly having to confront whiteness in both the research environment and the academy that at times is oppressive and debilitating? How then do I negotiate and balance my own interests and research agendas with those of my research participants? It is apparent that some white criminologists I have met when researching black people never account for their subjective whiteness or demonstrate any understanding of their participants' blackness. If any researcher focuses purely on the research outcomes, without understanding the 'by-products' that emerge from any interactions, then important insights might not be gained and in effect may be lost and be omitted from any findings. I would also argue that black research subjects generating and creating their own agency involves confronting what white society presents as both obstacles and aspirations. In doing so, it is hoped that they will further interrogate their own cultural contexts and examine how to transcend society's limited expectations of them. This dilemma in my view is where black crime fiction writers have more freedom and latitude than the impositions of whiteness masquerading as ethics in the research domain. The following auto-ethnographic account characterizes my work and speaks to those excluded, marginalized, and neglected criminologists who feel, as I do, that our voices should be heard more.

The extract below it taken from my ethnographic field notes during the August 2011 riots in England.

Extract from *Pause for a Minute: Reflections on the 2011 English Riots*

In Handsworth

I'm driving through Handsworth, on route to Birmingham city centre. There is an unusual calm in the air. People go about their daily business. The inner city landscape I'm familiar with has been altered slightly, as boarded up shops stand alongside the refurbishment of looted businesses. In spite of returning back to some normality, the scars of the previous few days are there if you know where to look. To the untrained eye it appears as though everything is operating as normal. However, there are cautious and fearful looks coming from older people as a group of young men wearing hooded tops walk past. Everyone is visibly uncomfortable and they seem to be operating with trepidation in case anything kicks off. Memories of the last few days come flooding back as I observe the restless body language and shuffles of passers-by, trying to avoid people walking their dangerous dogs. Defiant stares exchanged between the young and elderly keeps everyone on red alert. There is an uncomfortable awkwardness of a large group of commuters huddled together at a bus stop, hoping the bus will arrive soon.

My testimony could easily be mistaken for a work of fiction, highlighting that at times we are tellers of the stories we observe. Operating as a criminologist means gaining acceptance, approval, and permission from sections of the community who occupy the world of the streets. Every criminologist needs to know and understand black life that leads to black criminality, but fear may cause many of my white colleagues to avoid entering the world of the streets. I am not talking about holding focus groups in comfy constructed spaces, or handing out questionnaires in the safety of a classroom, or sitting in the comfort of an office, tape recording someone who has signed up to your research. I am talking about dialogue that takes place in shopping centres, barber shops, bookies, car parks, street corners, and other locations within the confines of the inner cities. Those I frequently come into contact with are gang members and ex-gang members. Others maybe have just been released from prison. Or it could be a mother wanting insights into her son's challenging behaviour or faith leaders who need to find ways of welcoming ex-offenders back into the congregation. In essence, you are on tap constantly, when the community sees you as someone they can go to, as well as wanting your insights into the pressing problems of the day. As a student and passionate consumer, I have observed in my readings how the lines between black crime fiction and black criminology are blurred, inform each other, produce productive authentic insights that stand alone, but are connected by the same conditions as circumstances. Prominent urban ethnographer Elijah Anderson (1990), writing in his book *Streetwise*, presented the following ethnographic note:

> On a Saturday morning in May at approximately 11.00, a young black woman was managing a little girl of three, a boy of about five, and a small boy in a stroller. They were standing at Linden Avenue and Cherry Street in the Village waiting for the bus. Two young white woman and a middle aged black man, apparently from the Village, were waiting for the bus too. The two small children began to fight over a toy. The older child won, and the smaller child began to have a temper tantrum. She wailed and stamped. Her face contorted, the mother cursed at the children, yelling obscenities at them and trying to get them to behave themselves. As the woman spanned the three year old, one of the white women visible cringed, as if to say to her friend and anyone else caring to pay attention 'oh! What a way to treat your child. Meanwhile the other white woman didn't say a word. The black man, in silence simply observed the performance. The woman continued to berate the children. She clearly had her hands full. Finally the bus arrives. (1990: 213)

Clearly, Anderson has an eye for detail; this passage could be a paragraph in a novel. Similarly, Petry (1946), writing in her novel *The Street*, could similarly have written this section as an ethnographic study note:

> The train crept out of the tunnel, gathered speed as it left the city behind. Snow whispered against the windows. And as the train roared into the darkness, Lutie to tried figure out by what twists and turns of fate she had landed on the train. Her mind balked at the task. All she could think was, it was that street. It was that god–damn street. The snow fell softly on the street. It muffled sound. It sent people scurrying homeward, so that the street was soon deserted, empty, and quiet. And it could have been any street in the city, for the snow laid a delicate film over the sidewalk, over the brick of the tired, old buildings; gently obscuring the grime and the garbage and the ugliness. (1946: 436)

Both Anderson and Petry capture the vivid nature of the inner city, using fact and fictional language to paint the evocative scenes. Another example is McCoy (1999) who, while conducting an ethnographic study, *Black Picket Fences: Privilege and Peril Among the Black Middle Class*, describes one of her participants, Lance, in much the same way as the sharply observed characterizations of Charles Dickens:

> In Groveland, everybody knows Lance. He went to the local public schools; he and his siblings participated in activities at Groveland Park, and now their children also attend Groveland School and frequent the park. Lance's position in the neighborhood is more multifaceted than the narrow title 'gang leader' might imply. He is a father, uncle, neighbor and former classmate, and as was mentioned Lance has been a community activist participating in the successful effort to close down neighborhood liquor stores. (1999: 76)

McCoy's descriptions could equally have occupied the pages of a screenplay. Contrast this with a fictional depiction of a Harlem street in Rudolph Fisher's book *The Conjure Man Dies*:

> But all of Black Harlem was not thus gay and bright. Any number of dark, chill, silent side streets declined the relenting night's favor. 130th Street, for example, east of Lenox Avenue, was at this moment cold, still and narrowly forbidding; one glanced down this block and was glad one's destination lay elsewhere. Its concentrated gloom was only intensified by an occasional spangle of electric light, splashed ineffectively against the blackness, or by the unearthly pallor of the sky, into which a wall of dwelling rose to hide the moon. (1932: 1)

The extracts for me highlight that the line between the writer of black fiction and research is extremely blurred, which suggests that for criminologists researching the inner city, writing creatively may at times be a better option in terms of reach and impact outside of academia. It is such a paradox that led me to create my own fictional black hard-boiled detective Franklin – an intersection of race, criminology, and fiction brought together to explore the complexities, contradictions, and challenges associated with the contemporary understandings of crime that emerged by being constantly excluded from peer review journals, conference platforms, and elite criminological forums. An example is Mark Fisher's article in *Sight and Sound* magazine written in 2012 when recounting his encounter with the Black Audio Film Collective's *Handsworth Songs*. Made for the Channel 4 series 'Britain: The Lie of the Land', the film *Handsworth Songs* was released in 1986, a year after riots in Handsworth, Birmingham, and Tottenham. Fisher argues that one of the striking things about *Handsworth Songs* is that when reactionaries once again feel able to make racist generalizations about 'black culture' in mainstream media, the collective's undoing of received ideas of what 'black' supposedly means remains an urgent project. In essence, black-driven narratives may succeed in their storytelling, in a way that many white storytellers telling black stories might fear to tread. As much as I love my US cousins writing on black crime fiction, I felt, as a criminologist, that I wanted to create a crime solver, who, like me, was a criminologist immersed in the black community. The essence of Franklin is contained within the stories of the 'shadow people', who are seldom credited for making the community a better place to live. It is also an examination of how, as a society, we must all be proactive in contributing to the development of future generations. Despite the bad press, the myths being talked about in the suburbs, and the outside impressions, the people of Franklin's world survive, like any other place, under siege. This is down to strong-willed and determined individuals, like Franklin, who take a stand in an attempt to making sure the community will not succumb to the pressures heaped upon them. Franklin is not about retribution or glorifying the inner city experience. It is about reframing our understanding of crime, not from the point of view of the forces of law and order, the courts, or prisons, but through the eyes of Franklin, a fictional gifted, but flawed, criminal defence QC turned private detective. Once revered and renowned as a pillar of the judiciary, Franklin exposes the holes in the system he once held dear, as well as journeying through his own personal odyssey where he has to engage with those he previously defended and prosecuted. At its heart, Franklin is about people, hope, dreams, and survival. Below is an unpublished extract of Franklin's opening monologue:

> My name is Edwin Joshua Franklin. People know me simply as Franklin. I'm black, mid 50s, and pro-black. I used to be a top barrister, but beating the shit out of the guy that killed my 5-year-old son Nathan broke me, my marriage, and caused me to play a hip-hop beat on the murderer's skull. I called it natural justice, but the judge didn't see it that way. I did 9 years, 3 months, and 2 days, and got out. I now live

in Stoneway, a tough inner city neighbourhood where my disillusionment with the criminal justice system brings me into conflict with the forces of law and order, corrupt local politicians, who want to criminalize the community I love. In spite of its problems Stoneway is a bustling and vibrant place to live. It's got the usual mix of problems, urban sprawl, and excitement, inhabited by a diverse multi-racial community, doing all they can to survive against the odds. And in spite the lack of political will to bring resources into the community, there is a cluster of activity, which has become a life line, for those who go about their normal lives, regardless of the crap around them. For me Stoneway is a place of barbershops, dumplin' shops, street corners, bassline's, black vernacular, and love. To my critics who want me to disengage from my close proximity to the black community because I used to live a privileged life, I say piss off! The community where I live has no voice. When I was a practising barrister I talked to, engaged with, and interviewed many black defendants, some gang affiliated; some not; many suffered from the three ds; disaffection, disillusionment, and disconnection. Being a champion of the law as a black man was at times very wearing and frequently made me wonder if I could have done something different that would have made me happier. I edit situations, which I know will affect me adversely. I have learnt how to listen to myself and try to act on what I hear. I knew that I must forgive myself and not carry the burden of guilt that for so long has weighed me down. I cannot change the past but I can affect the future by drawing on those valuable life lessons that only make sense when age and wisdom collide, forcing me to take stock of the precious time I've been given on this earth. I'm not bitter about what my life has been about, but accepting that life is about up and downs, and accepting what is given to you has at times been extremely challenging. My parents are now both dead, so emerging questions cannot be answered. I know I must now step into the light and become the person my mother knew I was, the person who people around me see, the person that many cannot or will not see, and those who when they do see it are intimidated. I've played a flawed character in a comic tragedy written and directed by others. In some respects I have been content to play minor roles in my own life, and occasionally play the lead. Always miscast but content to play the trickster, I have concealed a deeper longing to play my authentic self. None of this would have been possible if my current partner Marcia had not stuck with me steadfastly through my self-doubt. She encouraged me, worked with me, challenged me, and more importantly through the power of love, made me realize that it was my duty to do the right thing by reconnecting to those I thought had left me behind.

Franklin has given my work a new impetus as I now have a vehicle from which to explore those things that academia has attempted to impede. Franklin takes place in the darkness, set among the underworld of the night-time economy, symbolic of a dark pantomime that fuels much of the current voyeurism associated with the perception of crime itself, as reflected here by one of the greatest black hardboiled crime fiction writers of all time, Chester Himes. Himes wrote *The Real Cool Killers* with one of the earliest examples of having two black detectives work together in the New York City police force. Both 'Grave Digger Jones' and 'Coffin Ed Johnson' are brilliantly drawn from someone who understood the streets, the world of black detectives and the brutality they faced and meted out in equal measure:

> He parked directly in front of the Dew Drop Inn and pushed Ready through the door. On first sight it looked just as he has left it; the two white cops guarding the door and the colored patrons celebrating noisily. He pushed Ready between the bar and the booths, toward the rear. The varicolored faces turned towards them curiously as they passed. But in the last booth he noticed an addition. It was crowded with teenagers, three school boys and four school girls, who hadn't been there before. They stopped talking and looked at him intently as he and ready approached. Then at sight of the bull whip all four girls gave a start and the young dark faces tightened with sudden fear. He wondered how they'd got past the white cops at the door. (1975: 13)

Franklin is not about (re)hashing old stereotypes, but to closely examine the complexities associated with (re)presenting contemporary understandings of crime in its widest context through fiction.

Transcending boundaries

Among the earliest black detective novels are Pauline Hopkins' *Hagar's Daughter* (1901) and John Bruce's *The Black Sleuth* (1908). Rudolph Fisher is credited with writing the first novel with a black detective with only black characters *The Conjure Man Dies* (1932), while Ann Petry's 1946 debut novel *The Street*, which sold more than a million copies, became the first novel by an African-American woman. Willard Motley's novel *Knock on Any Door* appeared in 1947 to critical acclaim; he also had his works adapted into Hollywood movies. Hughes Allison (1948) similarly gained international acclaim with an attack on the stereotype of the black detective with the creation of African-American sleuth, Joe Hill. Chester Himes followed, using the detective novel to criticize racist practices as well as examine class issues and violence in Harlem. Himes was the first to introduce the hardboiled tradition in black detective fiction. In some ways, just as south central Los Angeles does in the fiction of Walter Mosley, the ghetto itself becomes as important as plot and character. Through his descriptions of Harlem streets, his emphasis on the black community and its vibrant use of language and music, Himes created a rich cityscape that illustrates the complexities of African-American culture. The writers, many of them women in the last 25 years, have shown how black detective fiction can reach a new and wider audience as their stories comment on a tradition of mainstream detective writing in America, while continuing aspects of the black detective tradition, and comment effectively on issues of race, class, and gender. Black British writers such as Mike Phillips, Courttia Newland, Dreda Say Mitchell, and Pete Kalu, have all made sizeable contributions in this area, but again have a lack of visible profile within so-called mainstream publishing of crime fiction. Ironically, the position of fictional characters having to navigate white spaces, even when operating outside them, is all too familiar for criminologists like me who study the connectivity between race and crime.

Black crime fiction as speculative fiction about crime

A possible way forward is for black crime fiction emerging from criminologists to be located within the speculative fiction genre of Afrofuturism, a cultural aesthetic and philosophy that explores the developing intersection of African diaspora culture with technology. Kodwo (2003) argues that Afrofuturism is a move away and an answer to the Eurocentric perspective that renders the history of African peoples invisible. Kodwo further argues that future-looking black scholars, artists, and activists should not only reclaim their right to tell their own stories, but also to critique those who have erased the contribution of black scholars, writers, and artists – past, present, and future. It is now, as Kodwo asserts, that there needs to be a challenge to the false authority of privileged academia as the sole interpreters of black lives and, more importantly, black futures. It could be argued that politicized black researchers may offer their own agency to the subjects of their inquiries, who have traditionally felt powerless and subordinate to visual storytelling through film and TV formats by informing and guiding. It is my wish that black crime fiction will involve coproduced relationships between criminologists, communities, and creatives where they will further interrogate their own cultural contexts and examine how to transcend society's limited expectations of them. The privileging of narratives from black people involved in crime is about engaging those individuals with a set of differences that are shaped by a range of situations, context, and experiences, race being only one such facet of their lives.

Reflection

I now find myself at an impasse when confronting the neglect paid to the racialization of crime by so-called mainstream criminology. Black crime fiction for me brings the reader into the world of the characters, reveals them as three-dimensional beings, who are complex and contradictory, struggling with making a decent living, all working alongside a failing social structure that struggles with making things better for people in the world of the community being portrayed. Maybe black fiction writers should choose to pursue fiction more than criminology, where the need to defend their academic racial existence is drastically reduced. It may be that black crime fiction offers criminologists a lesson in understanding the streets before making outlandish claims about black people and the communities they come from. By relocating black fiction within the speculative fiction genre, it will create space, not just a revision of crime fiction as a whole, but give black, indigenous, and progressive scholars a platform from which to engage wider society in a dialogue that is open, transparent, and insightful, free from the monopoly of so-called mainstream criminology. Interestingly enough, the next chapter follows in the same vein. The first time I encountered the works of Amri Baraka, Ntozake Shange, and August Wilson, I was starting out as a young activist. Theatrically I was introduced to black characters on stage for the first time. In their staging I escaped into a world that I knew, a world that was familiar, in spaces where I was not looked at. These experiences were then followed by my engagement with the theatre of apartheid, which motivated me to see theatre as an important part of my own struggle when engaging black offenders. It is to that work I turn now.

Provocation

How do you respond to the understanding that black crime fiction conveys important insights that can be used to aid learning about the racialization of crime and criminal justice?

4

Staging the Truth: Black Theatre and the Politics of Black Criminality

Chapter summary

This chapter aims to explore my use of applied theatre when working with black offenders. DeFranz and Gonzalez (2014) argue that notions of black performativity should assist black people in deciphering the varying degrees of contemporary blackness that now demands new meanings are brought to the fore. Like DeFranz and Gonzalez, I believe that we must stand our ground by contesting and challenging limited definitions that try to supress notions of embodied and performed blackness within criminal justice settings, and in those spaces where black offenders can negotiate embodied practices designed to heal and transcend those oppressive forces that compel many black offenders to reoffend. DeFranz and Gonzalez conclude by demanding we uncover the history of black performance by reclaiming those mechanisms used to root blackness and the black presence within it. So how does applied theatre respond to those needs pertaining to incarcerated black people?

Some of the greatest moments in my creative life have been as a dramatist and theatre director. It is also true that many of my most important teachable moments emerged from watching and studying the iconic theatre of August Wilson, alongside the uncompromising theatrics of Amiri Baraka, who both chronicled black life unapologetically, with beautiful dramatic brush strokes unimpeded by the expectations of society. Their dramatic works have created a route map into understanding the oppression of black people and its relationship to criminality based on a black condition shaped by a history of racial subordination. Equally as important is in the role played by applied theatre, which has enabled me to tell the real stories concerning black criminality, the plight of black offenders, the communities they came from, and the victims they have affected. Applied theatre, in this context, is a term that defines theatre that operates beyond the traditional and restrictive nature of Western theatre forms. It is characterized by work that deliberately engages in spaces with groups of people excluded, marginalized, or rendered invisible within the so-called mainstream theatre landscape. Applied theatre laid the foundation for me to bring the lived experiences of black offenders to a heightened prominence, providing a voice and an embodied space from which to explore issues traditional criminologists have feared or avoided to engage with on account of art not being scientifically robust enough.

Where are we now?

The historical conundrum that belied black British theatre is one where white producers selected and staged plays of the black experience with little attention, discussion, or engagement with the diversity of black theatre practitioners themselves. In the early 1980s, when I began to be actively involved in the black British theatre movement, I can attest that much of what we did was located in what would be best described as 'protest theatre'. Ironically, it was white funders and benefactors who enabled us to function, tenuous as those relationships to white infrastructures were. Seldom did we have a long run of our work, or a sizeable cast from which to stage epic productions. Tired of this situation, I turned my attention to working in prisons. Although the resources were scarce, the platforms were not. There were just too many prisons and black offenders to work with. It was during my early years working in prison theatre that something within me was awoken. I wanted to bring the experiences of black offenders to wider attention. Alas, most of what I produced stayed within the confines of prison, as the movement towards occupying the so-called mainstream of the British theatrical landscape meant that the work I was doing was pushed further into the background.

Who engages who?

Conquergood (2013) insists that performance studies scholars must continue to engage critically against the bias of Western intellectual systems by deploying performance as a lever to decentre without discarding and displacing the dominant cultures epistemological claims. In principle, Conquergood's positon may sound admirable, but the politics of black representation of black British theatre meant that the stories of incarcerated black people were not that significant in the grand scheme of things. Therefore, I took the position that deconstruction politically, socially, and culturally was the only way for me to go. I knew the consequences of doing so, but it was something I accepted as part of my journey and desire to bring transformative experiences to incarcerated black offenders. Ugwu (1995) sees that the expression of blackness through performance around the political concerns of identity and the need to be seen as human tends to be viewed from the margins, which dislocates the wider narrative of black people's own stories located where they are the centre of their universe. No more was that apparent than when working with black offenders, whose negative labels at times seemed to discount them from being seen as human by the mere fact they are seen as law-breakers. Applied theatre, therefore, not only provided the opportunity to explore self-reflection but, more importantly, to investigate the scope for transforming individuals into a new constructed self.

Culturally sensitive research methods

The negative portrayal and labelling of black people both within society and the wider criminal justice system can mean they are at times unable to find a place to be respected and validated. Hence crime becomes a way of getting back at a society that rejects them. Therefore, central to any rehabilitative process for black people should be to make sense of their world and organize it, in a way that will enable them to reframe their social reality, conducive to new dreams, desires, and concerns. By examining colour-blind or race-neutral perspectives within prisons, I examined through applied theatre the unspoken landscape of human and social relations distorting racial discourse and preventing awareness of knowledge that already exists in the real lived experiences of incarcerated black people. Hill–Collins (2000) argues that strengthening notions of self-definition as a way of challenging and eradicating stereotypical assumptions is an important consideration for black offenders who want to improve their lives. hooks (2004) likewise sees the understanding of black offenders' stories as a position and place of resistance that needs to be navigated if they are to liberate themselves from an oppressed social position. It may be that black offenders may have to reframe and name what is right for black offenders. Using culturally sensitive approaches such as applied theatre, Denzin (2003a) argues could succeed in creating space where black offenders will be hear their own stories, and the stories of others. Over the years, facing constant barriers, I struggled with using conventional theatrical approaches while working in prison. And then I discovered the work of Augusto Boal and encountered the understanding of theatre as praxis.

Theatre as praxis

> Praxis is a commitment to human well-being, the search for truth, and respect for others. It is the action of people who are free, who are able to act for themselves. (Carr and Kemmis, 1986: 190)

Boal encouraged critical thought about social conditions using theatre as the conduit and developed the 'Theatre of the Oppressed'. Over the years, much of my own work in criminal justice, public health, and education has built on his creative and philosophical ideas, which have in turn informed the direction of my future work. Similar to Boal, I believe that those of us who are engaged in critical inquiry should utilize performative approaches when conducting research that is socially and culturally driven. This approach serves as a tool for both maximizing the potential of research that affects people's lives, alongside increasing the potential impact in relation to personal, community, and social transformation/change. Working as a researcher I have observed how both quantitative and qualitative research reports tend to be disseminated mainly through traditional means – conferences, seminars, workshops, etc – where the format is quite predictable and, at times, some of the important messages, insights, and understandings can and do get lost in translation. In my view, it weakened the research as a whole if the feedback-sharing was relegated to mere sound bites or small chunks of information that only raised awareness.

Dramatizing research

To counter this position I began to explore dramatizing my research, so that it could be experienced through observation, active participation, and interaction. As a dramatist, I have been fortunate enough to have had many of my ideas produced for the stage, screen, and radio. Similarly, my academic work has been enhanced by using 'creative approaches' in the dissemination of my research. The need to dramatize research, therefore, was a 'call to arms' for all those who want to ensure that the work we do is connected to the widest constituency of influence and impact. Before, during, and after my doctoral studies, I had encountered many of my colleagues who were, and are, looking for a creative outlet for their own research as they want to reach a bigger audience, and to generate impact beyond the confines of academia, the report or dissertation/thesis. Therefore, I decided to create something for the voices contained within the research to be seen and heard. This decision was arrived at based on how I have extensively used drama in a variety of contexts and situations where my techniques and methods became a major pedagogical tool. The need for black offenders' research to reveal their own truths and to tell their own stories became a priority. In responding to issues of power and inequality I further called for the construction of counter-narratives that would enable the subordinated voices of black offenders or their community to both narrate and interpret their lived reality through the dramatization of their stories. To do so, I needed to employ a method of lifting their silences and bringing the unspoken to the surface. It was then I discovered the 'silences' framework'.

Silences

Serrant-Green (2010) developed the 'silences framework' to reflect elements of the research process where voices, experiences, insights, and understandings of the social world are rendered absent or invisible. 'Silences' derive from anti-essentialist viewpoints that accept that reality is neither objective, nor fixed; rather, the social world is constructed and determined by human beings in a particular society at a particular point in time. 'Silences', therefore, in this case, places value on black people's interpretations of events and their experiences as a key part of what they believe to be their truths in relation to the criminal justice system. Ultimately 'silences' are situated in the subjective experiences of black people and the social and personal contexts in which those experiences occur. It is often in the recounting of human experience and insight into research studies that the recognition of black people's 'silences' could make a unique and original contribution to the evidence base where previously it has been rendered invisible. Criminology all too often finds some kind of satisfaction by using research as part of an 'othering process' that is somehow designed to reveal deep insights and understandings of people's lives, based on the objectivity of the researcher, conducting research where they 'jump in' to communities, and then 'jump out' once they have found what they are looking for.

Transformation

A key goal when researching with black communities who themselves are oppressed is how the researcher assists in the transformative experiences associated with social justice. To transcend the confines of the ivory tower, I heeded the 'call to arms' by exploring the interconnection between critical inquiry and social justice using theatrical devices such as applied theatre. I wanted to probe how accessing the silences of incarcerated black people using applied theatre could reveal something new about the racialized experiences of black people within the criminal justice system as a whole. I wanted to access those silences to form the backdrop through which I could view the systemic way black people have been stigmatized and disproportionally represented, within criminal justice systems. In addition I wanted to expose how those experiences may be differently experienced in ways that were seldom heard. This required me to be able to utilize an approach to conducting studies that centralizes the sensitive or marginalized nature of the research in order to appraise criminal justice policies. Serrant-Green sees silences as those viewpoints that are not openly said, heard, or evidenced in the available (mainstream or easily accessible) bodies of literature related to the lived reality of incarcerated black people. Privileging the voices of incarcerated black people in this way would then create new and reframed life events that have meaning and significance rooted within a symbolic, metaphoric, and allegorical context. I decided that silences could best be articulated using 'ethnodrama' as the conduit. Ethno-drama played a significant role in achieving this goal, and consists of dramatized, significant selections of narrative collected through interviews, participant observation field notes, journal entries, and/or print and media artefacts (Saldana, 2005).

Applied theatre and me

The following abridged extract is taken from *Prison Theatre: Perspectives and Practices*, edited by James Thompson (1998). My chapter was entitled 'Silent Voices: Working with Black Inmates – A Perspective':

> Ever since I started working in prisons, I have pondered why I put myself through such an experience which at times is fraught with contradiction, pain and conflict. I am neither liberal nor someone who condones behaviours where people get hurt. I also do not see myself as a black community leader who needs to get even with the system.

It is quite basic, there is something within me which sees the potential in the most dissaffected individuals, and I feel that can offer a few outlets for self-examination and creative expression, leading to possible ways of finding solutions to becoming people who contribute to the overall well-being of society. Working with black inmates in not a joyride and should not be seen as a personal crusade or a liberal statement of reform. At times it can be unrewarding and scary. So much rests on your temperament, attitudes and beliefs. Prison creates a strong irony; on the one hand it is exhilarating, but at the same time it is a fearful place to be. Prison is made up of many constituent communities, black inmates being just one. The role of black artists working in prison is also one that is fraught with problems, as by default they are oppressive white institutions. (Thompson, 1998: 171)

This short extract highlights the several reasons why many of my contemporaries did not venture into the dark landscape of prisons. Firstly, there are accolades when working with black offenders and, secondly, there were many different fronts that theatre practitioners chose to operate from. In spite of the difficulties I faced, I was successful in producing and staging many powerful co-produced applied theatrical works with incarcerated black people. How then can the racialized experiences of black people within the criminal justice system shape a new worldview and ultimately their motivation towards desistance as an agency choice be expressed through theatre? It could be argued that to fully understand those experiences, they must be located and situated within the dramatic expression of the stories of black people involved in the criminal justice system that has been impacted on by racism, colour-blindness, white privilege, and black invisibility. This narrative would then form the backdrop through which we can view the systemic way black people have been stigmatized, over-represented, disproportionality represented within criminal justice systems. This narrative in its construction would be seen as a counter-narrative to the wider mainstream narrative that excludes and subordinates black people within the criminal justice system. This theatrical counter-narrative then becomes an important way of validating and naming black people's own reality. This in effect means that the theatrical expression becomes a catalyst for politicizing the struggle, not just for black offenders' desire to desist, but more importantly as part of their wider campaign for social and racial justice. I then discovered the groundbreaking work of eminent ethnodrama specialist Professor 'Johnny Saldana' from Arizona State University.

Ethnodrama and me

Ethnodrama is used to create a space that enables a subordinated individual to both 'narrate' and 'interpret' real-life events in the form of a counter-narrative. By doing so, that same individual can bring coherence and validation to their lives. Simply put, this is 'dramatizing the data'. In doing so, ethno-dramatic representations and presentations of incarcerated black people's understandings of the racialization of crime and criminal justice would bring their insights and understandings to a more heightened prominence. Denzin (2010) suggests that at the beginning of a new century it is necessary to re-engage the promise of qualitative research as a form of radical democratic process. We know the world only through our representations of it (2010: 6). This research would usually start from an interpretivist perspective – that is, the research focused on the meanings that incarcerated black people gave to their lived experiences (McAdams, 1985) exploring their own stories, adapted in 'dramatic form'. Denzin (2010) concludes by arguing that performative social science paradigms may provide some new answers to old problems – in this case improving the life chances for black men struggling to reintegrate into a community where their opportunities are blocked and they are denied access to the social structure that subordinates them. Likewise, Becker (1963) argues that in any system of ranked groups, participants take it as given that members of the highest group have the right to define the way things really are. Becker highlights why groups, such as men, must speak for themselves, to avoid assumptions that define a reality that 'will be partial and distorted in consequence' (1963: 241). McAdams (1988) maintains that abstinence from criminal activity requires ex–offenders to make sense of their lives in the form of a life story or self-narrative, and sees the use of theatre as a tool for both understanding and theorizing notions of both re-entry and desistance. It enables the naming of one's own reality as a way of preserving 'psychic self-preservation', thereby legitimizing one's experiences. Brazilian educator Paulo Freire points out that the 'oppressed' are better placed at times to understand their oppression, and argues their voices must 'speak' and 'be heard'. Similarly, eminent sociologist Norman Denzin points out that for 'subordinated and oppressed voices' to be heard, they must be assisted in their desire to transcend their silences. No more is the need to bring a subordinated voice to the fore than black people languishing on death row. I have been corresponding via letters with Al Cunningham, who was sentenced to death in 1989 for a murder committed in 1985, for over 20 years. Al has quietly reflected on his time on death row and agreed to me adapting his letters into an ethnodrama as a way of educating the wider public about the experience of being on death row. It was to this end that I created *Blue Sky at Midnight*.

Blue Sky at Midnight

Synopsis
Blue Sky at Midnight is a powerful (jazz hip-hop) poetic rendition of a reflection on the death penalty and its impacts on the human spirit. It is the story of a man separated by history, connected by punishment, and impacted by incarceration. *Blue Sky at Midnight* is not about contesting the need for punishment of crimes committed. Nor is it an attempt to justify criminal behaviour as an acceptable social norm. However, Al languishes on Death Row, based on a criminal justice system where the principle of 'retribution', not 'rehabilitation' reigns supreme. *Blue Sky at Midnight* therefore poses some important moral questions; namely 'whose lives do we privilege?' and 'whose lives do we punish? told in Al's own words. In doing so my role as a researcher was not to analyse his story but instead let him speak for himself, with me shaping his narrative in dramatic form.

Characters
Al Cunningham
Narrator

*Dark stage. A small prison cell and a large screen dominate the space. A hip-hop beat punctuates the moment. A shadowy figure wearing a mask, enters from opposite sides of the space, carrying a large lit candle. The figure moves outside his cell and removes their mask to reveal **Al Cunningham**, an African American death row inmate. He scans the audience, and freezes. **The Narrator** enters dressed in a court Jester's outfit. The Narrator's presence is felt but goes unseen by **Al**.*

Montage: criminal justice through the ages
17th-century crime and punishment
18th-century crime and punishment

19th-century crime and punishment
20th-century crime and punishment

Narrator: First person accounts from offenders
                Are often distorted 'N' misunderstood
                As simply a *'record of events'*
                Deemed what's bad 'N' what's good
                Many theories are created 'N' generated
                'N' at times are flawed 'N' conflated
                By those who should be challenged,
                Contested, discredited 'N' not exonerated
                Those responsible for this confusion
                Present an illusion, merged with delusion
                Where the production of new knowledge
                Promotes an oppressive *'zone of exclusion'*
                For many progressive scholars
                'N' indeed offenders themselves
                These views differ, are made invisible
                Confined to history 'N' sit on university
                    shelves
                (Walks away and watches on from a vantage point
                *away from **Al**, who retreats to his cell and throws*
                a ball repeatedly against his cell wall)

***Al**'s cell is very small, brooding, with just a bed, small TV, and a small table for company. **Al** stares out the window, lets out a loud scream and jumps to his feet where he stares at the audience with menace.*

Montage: capital punishment
Guillotine
Firing Squad
Hanging
Electric Chair
Lethal Injection

Al: I am a death row inmate, waiting to be killed
                by the state. Since my incarceration many
                members of my family have died. Chained
                and shackled, I was taken away from my
                family, shipped, stripped, stacked and packed
                into a small cell. I am now paraded in front

of observers whose eyes penetrate with their stares of, lust, and hatred. I am stigmatized and placed in solitary confinement. I endure all this, day after day, month after month, and year after year. My mother a very intelligent, well-educated woman is now growing old and sick. My daughter misses me, her father, and does not understand the circumstances of my incarceration. Both of them continue to support and love me. Like me they are trapped within an emotional prison enduring the same pains and psychological taxations as I am. My cell is 4 feet wide, 10 feet long, and 8 feet high. My bunk, sink, and toilet are made of stainless steel. I can lay down with my shoulder pressed against one wall and reach out and touch the other wall without straightening my arm. The food slot is directly in front of my bunk where I can reach up and accept the food being slid in. I have a TV sitting on two cardboard boxes. Whilst at the end of the bunk is the toilet. I have a typewriter sitting on two cardboard boxes in the centre of the cell.

We are not allowed to work

We have to stay in our cells for 23 hours
    a day.

We become stagnant

We are alone with ourselves.

We are denied every human right

We are disrespected, denied, and rejected,

We are stripped and degraded at any
    given time

Our personal belongings are constantly
    searched

Thrown into a pile and stepped on

Our mail is scanned, searched, and
rejected

Fear is always just around the corner.

My incarcerated home is a world of violence and hostility. I try desperately to find something positive, mentally encouraging,

or just something that will sufficiently
sustain a reason to remain sane in this
monstrosity where I am not considered a
human being,
I have suffered from the hands of torturers.
I have felt the pain go deep into my body
I have been beaten so much and badly
I doubt the soundness of my instincts
So many thoughts circulate through
my mind.
So many unpleasant experiences
Monsters creating new monsters
Where intellect is regarded as a threat
And violence is the highest form of
communication.
*(Al drops to the ground and proceeds to do press
ups in a regimented and vigorous fashion)*

Montage: incarceration
Native American Reservation
Victorian Jail
Prison Yard
Inner City Ghetto

Al: *(To audience)* I've seen many break, both
            mentally and physically. Under the hard
            hickory-wood clubs of sadistic guards,
            personalities change, tender people become
            twisted, silent brooding figures, lost in the
            shadows of bars. Never being able to get
            out, they begin to smell bad. Few prisoners
            get better in these overcrowded compounds.
            Often their psychosis gets worse as they are
            beaten. They never change, never worse,
            never better, for year after year. There are
            many nights I've laid awake, listening to the
            sounds of the night, wishing I were someplace
            else. Listening to the sounds of car horns,
            babies crying, construction workers making
            irritable noises, and above all, experiencing
            the freedom I so desperately crave. The night
            is so still, I can almost hear the dreams of

others as they lie sleeping on their steel cots dreaming their dreams, as the night moves on. The hours pass slowly, but then, before you realize it, it is the dawning of a new day. Once again, I will be forced to listen to the obnoxious yells and screams of others as they hold their nonsense conversations. Some talking loud because they want to be noticed by others, they feel a need to impress others, they suffer from a deep feeling of lack of self-worth. Others, talking to cover up their fears, and gain strength from the rest. Then there are those who talk and make noise simply to hear the sound of their own voices. I'm tempted to think I am in some sort of insane asylum instead of a prison. So many times I have had to prevent myself from cheapening my character, depreciating and demeaning myself.

No encouragement
No inspiration
No hope
No self-discipline
No goals
No constructive plans
No retention span
No future
Bad habits
Unconscious physical habits, vocal expressions,
Nerve disorders, inconsiderateness,
Lack of respect for others, mental blocks,
Psychological walls and character distortions
Mind and body stand still in time,
Frozen and suffocating from the lack of individuality,
Yet, I know I must endure,
1 must sustain,
I must survive,
I must maintain myself
And hope that one day
I will be free

(Al throws himself to the floor, rocks from side and then stops abruptly. He takes a deep breath, followed by manic laughter erupting into uncontrollable tears)

Montage: 19th-century crime and punishment

The Treadmill
Walking the Yard
The Crank
Blindfolds
Hanging

Al: Livin' on top of ...
            Livin' inside of ...
            Livin' outside of ...
            Myself
            I need space
            To hear myself
            Be near myself
            To know myself
            To be myself
            Claus ... tro ... pho ... bic
            At ... mos ... phere
            Always lingers
            Always there
            Depressed
            Obsessed
            My brain
            Suppressed
            I need to rest
            I feel so weak
            The landscape's bleak
            Can't reach my peak

Montage: the prison code

Men and Women behind bars
Prison Gangs
Attica Riots
Strangeways Riot
Dartmoor Jail (Victorian)

Al: Need to think
To breathe,
To med ... itate
I need more time
To con ... tem ... plate
I cannot stop
I cannot wait
What is my role?
What is my fate?
Why am I stoppin'
To hes ... I ... tate?
Where is this place?
Dark
So blue
I knew
This time
Would come,
Carrying this weight
A heavy load
Walking down this
Endless road
Winding ... spiraling
Bottomless well
Staircase to hell
Here's the news
Must refuse
To lock down
Push 'N' kick
Kick 'N' push
This rush
Of vibes inside
I scream
'N' I shout
Let it out
Let it out
There's now light
No more fight
Future's bright
I'm all right
It is a new day
I am a new me
We all need to let it out ...

Before it too late
Peace is what I need ...
*(Al retreats to his cell windows and stares with a fixed gaze. **The Narrator** stands at the entrances to both cells, looks at **Al** throwing the ball on the wall, before turning to face the audience)*

Narrator: Their narratives are made up of fragments
Of stories that inspire 'N' constrain
Every movement, every action,
What they experience is called 'strain?'
Each story motivate, highlight, or legitimize the harm
Can be told thru' raw anger or depression or thru' calm
Their stories evaluate, report, inform 'N' recount
'N' tell us about the motivations, intentions, 'N' the amount
Of experiences that reveals how the past shapes the future
Explores the dreams, visions, 'N' desires of nature versus nurture
Could be counter factual propositions or even anecdotal
Stories look at factors of desistance or behaviour that's anti-social

Montage: nighttime
Moonlight
Darkness
Sunrise
Lynched Bodies

(Staring at the night sky) As 'the' darkness of night slowly 'fades, the dawning of a new day reveals itself. I dread having to experience another day within this monstrosity. Yet I know I must survive and endure it. So as I raise my aching body, racked with pain and weak in strength. I go to the sink and wash away my individuality, my inner fears,

my needs, my desires and my dreams, and set them on the shelf till the night comes again and again and again. I then put on my convict mask and prepare myself for the unpredictable, the constant irritations, the slamming of gates, the firing of guns, the erratic and unstable behaviours of others. I then accept the daily reality that I must listen to 443 problems, of others like me. I know I must make it through this day so that I can have my night, to once again listen to the surrounding sounds of dreaming. At night I can then think, I can be me, and I too can then dream. Each time a person is executed killed, or dies on death row, a part of each inmate on the row also dies with him. The slow, meticulous march toward death which we each experience daily is far more uncivilized and criminal than the acts for which we are charged and eventually executed for.

(Paces erratically, moves his feet to a beat)

Lost in the abyss ... was stuck behind the door

Drowning in self-pity ... 'N' emotionally poor

Going thru' a re-birth with a spiritual placenta

I'm arriving at the crossroads ... the sign outside says enter

Like a broken jigsaw ... I am on the mend

This struggle cannot continue ... my struggle has to end

Need to change the pattern 'N' make some different choices

Tired of the cracked record ... need to hear some different voices

Know it's time to reclaim myself ... my broken wings must fly

Know it's time to climb the mountain ... no more asking why?

I am at the crossroads 'N' feeling overjoyed

Transition … transformation … then the filling of the void

Know I have shed a skin 'N' accept that I have now grown

Know this phoenix has risen 'N' a new seed has been sown

Love shouts very loudly … calling out my name

Cannot push it back anymore … coz I understand the gain

I'm walking past the crossroads … I'm excited as I enter

Spirit wraps its arms around me … I am glad that God has sent her

As the light shines thru' the darkness … I can now see clear

Once there was pure darkness … now there is less fear

Life's no longer a mystery … I understand the plot

Wisdom holds me gently … teaches me what is from what's not

No longer at the crossroads … the threshold has been breached

But the journey will continue … until the destination has been reached

No longer at a crossroads …

'N' I've now decided

It is time

Time to be me

(Retreats to the window and stares into space)

Montage: daytime

Winter

Spring

Summer

Autumn

Narrator: *(Stares at the audience with menace)* The narrative of the oppressed reveals participation 'N' consent

Order of how things happen 'N' how
freedom comes from dissent
Silent voices scream about deceit is used to
control 'N' prevent
expose the real motivation behind history's
'N' society's intent
passive tolerance sees harm done 'N' not just
that of the crime
Told as critical events that are sustained 'N'
maintained over time
We were understandings of legal 'N' not just
illegal acts
Are obscured from our gaze with exaggerated
empirical facts
Whilst, we're not told the stories
Behind the myths with openness 'N' sensitivity
Some stifle real progression
Going from inclusion into exclusivity
Stories reveal what is narrated and who
narrates 'N' what
What are the key factors in the story 'N'
also what it is not?
Characters 'N' metaphors 'N' the making
of meaning
Constructing new scenarios with emotion
'N' of feeling

Montage: human decline

Holocaust
Slavery
Apartheid
Reservations

Al: *(Slow and measured to the audience)* No one
desires to exist in this state, though with some,
it may be the only state of existence in which
they can function. If we are to ever reach
a state of rehabilitation and reconciliation,
then the circumstances surrounding our
existence within the prison environment
must drastically change to promote a positive
atmosphere for re-entry back into society.

You cannot deprive a person of their ability to maintain their hygiene. You cannot place a person within an environment which has inadequate heating and cooling systems, where he freezes in the winter and suffocates from the heat in the summer. You cannot throw poor quality meals together and classify it as food. You cannot force a person to exist within an environment of violence, living in constant fear, and deprived of family support. If you provide us with nothing but walls and bars, you then create a very frustrated and troubled human being. The death penalty is merely a source of retribution. It has not been shown that the death sentence is more effective to deter or prevent murder than the alternative sentence of life imprisonment would be. Today, politicians are encouraging the rush to executions. We are waiting to die, psychologically and physically. Those whose spirits have not been broken are sustained by the hope of eventually returning to society as free men and women.

(Throws himself to the ground and rocks gently with manic laughter)

Montage: families
Fathers and Sons
Mothers and Daughters
Grandparents
Family Gatherings

Montage: 10 bulls (Buddhist)

Al: The death penalty as a deterrent is meaningless. On death row we have one thing in common, we are poor and can't afford the high-powered attorneys. We are mostly economically deprived and raised in poverty. So many doors are closed to us. We grew up in poor neighbourhoods, where the majority had limited choices or opportunities to move out of the poverty trap.

*(Repeatedly throws the ball on the wall. **Al** erupts in a frenzied rage and throws the ball away. He lunges at the wall as if he wants to escape. Tired he flops to the ground. **The Narrator** speaks whilst pacing)*

Narrator: Stories are not static 'N' are open to full interpretation
multiple voices, change 'N' unfold, from death thru' to liberation
Stories co-produced, manufactured 'N' tailored to suit the occasion
Influenced by setting, environment 'N' arguments 'N' persuasion
Meaningful adaptations with selective reconstruction
Non-linear, sequential 'N' powerful, layered with deduction
We act upon our stories through language 'N' thru' power
Whether they're reciprocal or volatile in the telling we must scour
hidden meanings 'N' truths to find the emergence of new codes
Counter narrative's contest take us down new roads
Disputes emerge over dispelling common held beliefs
Challenging labelling, or toppling white collar chiefs
To liberate this narrative data must be found
Voices must be heard 'N' reflected in the sound
Of the telling 'N' the knowing 'N' the hearing of the story
In the pain 'N' in the suffering 'N' in the victory 'N' in the glory

Montage: death

Plants
Animals
The Ocean
Rainforest

Narrator: Characters 'N' the scenes 'N' the plots 'N'
twists 'N' turns
Endings 'N' beginnings 'N' the lessons we
must learn
In the truths we must seek 'N' the mission
'N' the quest
In the methods 'N' of our analysis 'N' in the
hypotheses we test
We must connect 'N' collaborate in the lives
with whom we share
We must never let their stories die, fade,
drown, or disappear
This narrative provides the arguments and
evidence of our truth
Which enables us to counter the lies with
our own historical proof
One man separated by history, connected by
punishment, and
impacted by incarceration. 'whose lives do
we privilege?' and
'whose lives do we punish?'

(A powerful hip-hop beat punctuates the moment.
***Al** exits. **The Narrator** exits)*
The End

Reflection

The importance of embodied practices using applied theatre with
black offenders is quite simple. It interrogates the barriers, pitfalls,
and triumphs associated with the racialization of the criminal justice
system and its impact on black offenders. The byproduct of engaging
with applied theatre processes is in theatre being used to enable the
move towards atonement and redemption possibilities as agency choices
required to assist the offender in considering restorative and other
rehabilitative choices, when navigating their desistance trajectories.

In my work with the National Trust for the Development of African-American Men, I used this approach within the context of a 'prison-based rite of passage' programme, where the objective was to use theatre as a way of delabelling black men who had lost a sense of identity by their continued investment in crime. Using applied theatre enabled me to assist the men from making a transition from labels such as 'offender', 'thug', and 'criminal', towards reclaiming a new identity as just 'men'. *Blue Sky at Midnight* has not only given insight to the trauma of languishing on death row but, more importantly, enabled wider society to understand more about Al as a human being. Ironically, as much as I love theatre as a way of engaging with the community, it is the black representation in film and TV that has a massive impact on my work with offenders. In contemporary society laced with screens, social media platforms, and a proliferation of new visual formats, the visual media in my view has so much to offer in the way we understand criminality in all of its various guises. As a criminologist, the depictions, portrayal, and narratives located in these mediums in the way black criminality is (re)presented not only provide ways to examine black involvement in crime, but also create valuable insights into the way in which these mediums construct black stereotypes that feed a white supremacist narrative. Therefore, a closer inspection of the racialization of crime in film and TV is relevant here.

Provocation

What thoughts do you have regarding the use of black theatre as a tool to examine black lives in relation to the racialization of crime and criminal justice?

Beyond *The Wire*: The Racialization of Crime in Film and TV

Chapter summary

This chapter explores considerations about black depictions and representation in relation to the racialization of film and TV formats. *Fast forward.* Watching George Floyd being murdered in front of my eyes on YouTube was no longer the domain of slickly produced TV and cinematic portrayals of police brutality. Like the Rodney King beating in 1991 and later the O.J. Simpson case in 1994, the visual spectacle of 'trial by media' has now been replaced by the equally distasteful 'trial by social media', where the general public, can shoot, edit, and upload crimes in real time. *Fast forward.* Dance group Diversity performed a routine inspired by Black Lives Matter on an episode of *Britain's Got Talent* in September 2020; complaints made to the media regulatory body Ofcom rose to over 20,000. Diversity's choreographed piece depicted a white police officer kneeling on the Diversity star and temporary *Britain's Got Talent* judge Ashley Banjo, echoing the killing of George Floyd in the US. The group all took the knee before the start of the song 'Black Lives Matter' by Dax, which included the lyric 'I can't breathe', the last words uttered by Floyd. Suddenly, the right to freedom of expression was under siege.

Whose cinematic representation is it?

Film and TV in contemporary society are important mediums that provide influential entertainment, insights, and values, that seep into society's consciousness. I remember the rapturous applause that greeted the arrival of the groundbreaking movie *Black Panther*, which depicted the African nation of Wakanda, a fictitious world occupied by black people. As much as I enjoyed the spectacle of seeing a predominantly black cast, with a wonderful cinematic representation of futuristic black life, I did not jump up and down with glee. For me, the cinematic portrayal of black lives in relation to the criminal justice system has seldom been portrayed accurately, sensitively, or with any great depth. Ta-nehisi Coates is the writer of the comic book series Black Panther, who also wrote a spinoff entitled *Black Panther and the Crew*, which got cancelled after a few episodes. However, the major success of the film would suggest it was the film industry that benefitted from the black super hero, and one of the originators of the project has been superseded by the Hollywood elite, who have commodified this important literary development, and sold it back to black people. Here, I posit that similar portrayals of black criminality on both film and TV at times undermines the important work of black criminologists and practitioners, who are sidelined while many white academics seize on 'race' without considering the authors of those narratives. More importantly, this position, I would argue, significantly enhances the maintenance of inaccurate portrayals of black criminality that fuel ignorance, that seep into the consciousness of a society, where those distorted narratives shape negative perceptions of black involvement and investment in crime. This chapter, therefore, aims to explore some of the tensions and contradictions associated with this conundrum.

Mediatized worlds, race, and crime

Cultural criminology calls for oppositional criminological scholarship, to dissolve conventional understandings and accepted boundaries within criminology itself. Some criminologists argue that neither criminological theory nor media theory can adequately lay claim to holding the answers to the complex nature of media activity in relation to crime, and are further critical of the lack of unification of those same respective disciplines. Although cultural criminology offers the possibility of locating wider debates around crime and the media where cultural dynamics interact with the practices of crime and crime control in contemporary society, race is distinctly absent. How then do contemporary criminologists undertake research in environments that are challenging, difficult, and risky? How do we gather data in mediatized worlds where crime operates online? The recent graphic depictions of beheadings posted online by ISIS, which was preceded by the extensive blog written by Norwegian mass murderer Anders Brevik, are further examples of how this mediated world is playing out. Equally as timely are the posed photographs on Facebook of Dylann Roof (2015), who shot nine African-Americans dead in a church in Charleston, South Carolina while standing next to the confederate flag. The murders of reporters Alison Parker and Adam Ward (2015), during a live broadcast, by Vester Lee Flanagan, who posted his own video of the shooting, suggests that mediated crime has moved way beyond the domain of the forces of law and order, state, and crime control. Instead, the mediatized world of crime is now being fuelled by a democratization of virtual space, driven by the wider public. It is, therefore, incumbent for all criminologists to transcend straightforward explanations and neat theoretical understandings of crime, and occupy the space outside the comfort zone of the 'ivory tower'. Instead, this is a historical moment that requires a move towards a more 'mediated criminological imagination', with a significant need to update our thinking on the racializing role of the media when investigating how these representations enhance or distort our understandings of black people's investment and involvement in criminal activity.

Contrast

The stereotype of the 'black ghetto' has long been exploited for commercial gain by film and TV companies. Here Ferrell et al (2008) argue that contemporary rap music embodies the evolving fusion of crime, consumerism, or transgression, and popular art. But the commodification of crime and corporate colonization of crime and violence today pervades popular culture as a whole. Ferrell et al in my view suggest that it is easier to exploit the victims of the condition that created the ghetto than address a deeper issue of white privilege and its ability to vacate spaces no longer required as a form of social cast-off for poor and disenfranchised communities such as black people. Cashmore (1997) further wades in, arguing that black culture has been converted into a commodity, usually in the interest of white-owned corporations; how blacks have been permitted to excel in entertainment only if they conform to white images of blacks; and how blacks themselves, when they rise to the top of the corporate entertainment ladder, have tended to act precisely as whites have in similar circumstances. How does this play out? Marriot (2005) sees the representation and portrayal of black hyper-masculinities as a counter-response to a society that attempts to pacify black men's need for validation and self-determination within a white society. Within cinematic portrayals, seldom do I observe black people involved in criminality responding to the condition they face as a causal factor. Instead, two-dimensional portrayals seldom contextualize those structural determinants that cripple and disable the ability for poor black people to actualize themselves in an economic environment that excludes them. Mauer (1999) similarly highlights how the criminal justice system has both labelled and incarcerated diverse black masculinities as an extension of US criminal justice policy following the legacy of historical sustainable white privilege. Hill-Collins (2005) also sees the interplay between the two dominant racialized masculine identities as the basis for keeping black and white men apart. Finally, Alexander (2010) sees the expression of 'colour blindness' within the criminal justice system as a way of operationalizing the marginalization and subordination of black men as a key underpinning factor that explains how mass incarceration in the US can be understood. It is this writer's view that racial caste in a time of globalization has not ended but has been merely redesigned within the context of the criminal justice system. Those aforementioned positions would suggest that many film and programme makers have little interest or investment in using these mediums to unpack the mechanics of oppression that shapes the disposition towards criminality and instead prefer to generate stereotype for profit. Gillespie (2006) too argues that art is determined by racialized constructs that lean too heavily on black existential life that is mostly debilitating. Gillespie further asks what notions of black cinematic representation and embodiment would be like if the visual world of black life transcended its lived reality. Gillespie further argues that notions of cinematic blackness should not focus on a form of racialized determinism, but instead be constructed in ways that respond to the dreams, hopes, and aspirations of black men, alongside the history of racial oppression that both shapes and sustains those perceptions. Gillespie sees any filmic representations of blackness as being rooted in historical contexts as a form of musical polyphony, where each part of the narrative of black men is produced in an intersectional lens, giving rise to differing and complementary melodies and harmonic expression that generates a new improved black male cinematic narrative. It would be that in the case of the black male image, stereotypical representations bolsters white supremacist beliefs.

Malevolence

Hutchinson (1994) argues that the image of the malevolent black male is based on a durable and time-resistant bedrock of myths, half-truths, and lies. Hutchinson further argues that to maintain power and control plantation owners held that black men were savages and hypersexual. Hutchinson's assertion leads me to believe that in spite of being positive, productive, well qualified, and law-abiding, I will still wind up in the firing line of racist stereotypes. Fanon (1952) argues that for black men to live with hatred as an intimate possession, this becomes part of a living nightmare for many black men. Fanon goes further by citing that the negative portrayal of black men through a form of racialized censorship pushes black men further into the cultural abyss. Fanon concludes by spelling things out clearly, remarking that distorted myths lead to black men attaining the self-fulfilling prophecy centring on violence and hopelessness fuelled by nihilistic behaviours. hooks (2004) sees black males who reject racist and sexist stereotypes as having to still cope with the imposition of negative labelling that has no relation to their real lives. hooks goes further to express the view that if black males are socialized not to attain socially acceptable goals, then they will turn to patriarchal coercive values that invariably leads to harming themselves and others. Curry (2017) posits that we should conceptualize the black male as a victim, oppressed by his sex, and sees the possibility of black males challenging the existing accounts of black men and boys desiring the power of white men who oppress them, which has been proliferated throughout much academic research across disciplines. Curry further argues that black men struggle with death and suicide, as well as abuse and rape, and their gendered existence deserves further study and investigation. Black theatre has always created a platform to enable black men such as me to explore my own sense of self in a world where my masculinity has been historically distorted and defined by others, much the same as feminist, intersectional, and indigenous scholars have argued.

The question

As a theatre practitioner I always dreamt about writing for film and TV and, in 1997, I achieved my objective by writing for BBC 1's flagship medical drama *Casualty*. Out of that experience I went to the US and worked on several film ideas, returning to the United Kingdom determined to pursue a career as a screenwriter. However, I quickly learned that the British TV and film industry was just another extension of the denied access I was used to. This chapter therefore explores how the limitations of my engagement with theatre as a medium in terms of impact and reach progressed into film and TV. The location of black criminality and victimhood at times in the medium of film and TV leans too heavily on black participation in crime as an individual act, without serious interrogation of the socio-historical context from which crime has emerged. On closer examination I began to realize that visual storytelling not only brings stories to a wider audience, but the advent of social media platforms is creating new ways of seeing black criminality that are no longer the sole domain of scholars, politicians, or historians. In spite of the success of TV shows like HBO's *The Wire*, the location of black criminality and victimhood tends to lean heavily on stereotypical and pathologized portrayals of black participation in crime. The constant toing and froing of this mis(re)presentation of black criminality has seldom been explored using TV and film viewed from a black criminological lens. Prominent African-American novelist Chester Himes poses a question:

> This is the voice of Negro heroes, dead on American fronts throughout all American history; the voice of Negro martyrs, dead, hung from American trees, the voice of centuries of Negro oppression in the unmarked graves of Negro slaves who prayed to God for freedom from birth to death; the voice of the centuries of contained waiting, repressed hoping, stained with the tears of bitterness that saw death before light, the voice that comes out of a bruised and beaten past, out of a confused and shadowed present, an obscure future, like a clarion it comes, loud, clear, positive, if you are a Negro American, you cannot fail to hear this voice. (1975: 213)

Where are those stories that Himes makes so plain in his statement? Where are the filmmakers who will be brave enough to create a mediatized counter-narrative that will contest what many film and TV depictions portray when it comes to the lived reality of the black presence in criminal justice? It may be that the lens through which we view black criminality needs to change.

Fact or fiction?

What is clearly evident and at work is how the visual media shapes and drives the narratives that wider society consumes and forms opinions about the subject of their investigations. TV shows like *The Wire* (2002–08) exemplified this assertion by using heightened realities of black life to generate both interest and audience ratings. *The Wire*, created by David Simon and Ed Burns and considered by many critics to be the best TV drama series ever made, was set in Baltimore. In spite of its critical success, I remember when it arrived in the United Kingdom it was destined to the graveyard shift on BBC 2, in the wee small hours. For me a valuable opportunity was lost to illuminate black life and its relationship to criminality in a way that had never been seen before. However, I would argue that the politics of *The Wire*, which traced corruption within the criminal justice system to the highest political office, may have been a risk that British broadcasters were not prepared to take. However, in 2014 I was fortunate enough to undertake a Winston Churchill Fellowship in the city of Baltimore, where I met some of the real people that *The Wire* was based on. My encounters with them required sensitive brokerage, knowledge of the streets, as well as moving beyond the TV show's depiction of their lived reality. Gaining access at times was at the discretion of criminals, gang members, or the 'credible messengers' (go betweens) I liaised with. The following extracts are from my research notes.

Black masculinities portrayed

Dr Ted Sutton was a reformed gang member and committed anti-violence campaigner. Here I describe our first encounter:

Ted

I'm picked up in a large car by Ted. Ted, a huge man, with an even bigger smile, greets me in a friendly and caring manner. As we drive off Ted begins to share his narrative, and reveals Melvin to be his mentor and close friend. I learn that Ted is an ex-strong arm man (Enforcer), who has participated in many acts of violence and crime, and like Melvin works on behalf of the community, as a gang mediator, mentor, and has a serious mission to save the lives of the hardest to access young men in Baltimore. Ted breaks it down in detail, from street warfare, gangs, crime, and more importantly how he found God. Ted talks about his family consisting of civil rights activists, members of the Black Panther party, and an array of powerful elders in his life all connected for changing people's lives. Ted tells me that being the middle child with an older and younger sibling pushed him into a life of darkness and crime. The multiple deaths of his friends, constant street battles, and fear of incarceration culminated in being acquitted in a profiled court case and undergoing a faith-based conversion all at the same time. The conversation is broken as we end up at a small apartment block. Ted tells me here is a young gang member who is in trouble and is looking to get out of the lifestyle. A young black emerges, climbs onto the van and exhales loudly as if in deep pain. A phone call brings bad news. This young man was not happy, but also suffering from a deeper sense of insecurity, as he feels that no one cares for him. Being face to face with this young gang member was at first quite frightening. Not because he was a gang member, but a young man who was in a volatile state of mind. Ted spoke to him for a while, calming him down with reassuring words and a soothing tone.

Iz was a serving gang member who was at the cusp of exiting his gang-affiliated life. It was Ted who had to vouch for me and negotiate with Iz to let me connect with him. Again, this is my first encounter with Iz.

Iz

I'm sitting in the passenger seat watching Ted enter the door of a small apartment. I'm quite nervous as I'm not too clear about what's going on. All I've been told is there's a young man wanting to get out of his gang, and he's in distress. I pan around trying to repress any anxious feelings that I have, but I keep returning to the White door that Ted has gone through. It's a bizarre feeling. I know Ted is a few feet away, but his absence makes me feel vulnerable. A few moments later Ted emerges and fills me in on his discussions with the young man inside the apartment. It transpires that this young man has a range of problems and is not coping. A gang member not coping means trouble if it's not sorted. Towards the end of Ted's briefing the door opens and out steps 'Iz', a small framed, light skin African American, in his early 20s. He is followed by his partner, who has a vexed look on her face. Clearly there is some tension between them. Iz takes a call, paces up and down, then terminates the call abruptly. He's pissed. Iz jumps into the back seat of Ted's car and lets out a scream. He's been told if he doesn't find $6000 for owed rent, then he will be evicted. In order to put some distance between himself and the gang, Iz decided a new start was in order. However, no job, qualifications, or experience, means he has no capacity to meet his obligations. What an irony. A gang member wants to turn his life around, but the available means to do so are not on offer to him. Iz's obvious distress becomes more intense out of the desperation of his situation. He wants to leave the gang, but if he can't get money for his rent, he may have to reconsider his position. Outsiders to his situation would say it's easy. The reality is far from true. Ted tries to calm the situation with seasoned wisdom and care. Iz listens, but the pain of this moment silences any responses he may give. I look at Iz's puffed up eyes, clenched fists, and body rocking, and felt compelled to talk to him. As was the norm in these situations Ted had to vouch for me, as a way of brokering any conversation I needed to have. Trust is the most important value for gang members. So the sight of a complete stranger like me creates a situation where that trust must be earned. Ted smiles at me and praises Iz for his interaction with me. The frown lines have gone, Iz looks less stressed, and any thoughts about gang life have disappeared. A call comes through. Iz retreats back to his gang demeanour. Iz touches my fist, exits the car, and ushers Ted into the apartment. I'm alone again. It feels like it's a long time, even though it's a matter of minutes. Ted and Iz emerge, embrace each other. It's time to go. I get out the car and thank Iz for his openness and vulnerability. We touch fists, I walk off. Iz calls me back and asks me for some contact details. I give him a card. We leave. Ted gets a text from Iz. He thanks Ted for introducing me to him. Ted smiles and tells me that my actions have not only assisted Iz, but I have averted a possible street robbery, based on his current situation. I felt good. Reality is you can't save everyone, but you can bring some relief to a difficult situation. Small steps make a big one.

Finally, we have one of the most important, and scary, encounters with a Baltimore gang member. This meeting was brokered by Ted.

Bloods

Night has descended, me and Ted are in a car park, face to face with a man sporting a red bandana. My first encounter with a member of the 'Bloods' gang is surreal, challenging, and insightful. Being granted an audience with him, followed by a meeting I will never forget was one of the most powerful experiences of my life. He was charismatic, intelligent, and truly a leader. The conversation did not focus on gangs, but more on fatherhood and society in general. The mixture of fear and exhilaration ran through my veins. This was no film set, it was real. 30 minutes later I was sitting in Ted's car, whilst he and 'the blood' talked. I observed Ted brokering, negotiating, and mediating with skill and commitment. I was truly impressed not only by Ted's unswerving commitment to trying to make Baltimore a better place, but the gang member's openness to reasoning and dialogue. Be under no illusion, any US gang member affiliated to the Crips and the Bloods is not a saint. However, they are men and fathers, who have made a choice that many find offensive, scary, and wrong. Be that as it may, they exist alongside us, occupying the same space, going to the same shops, taking their kids to school, and trying to survive in their own way. We can all have an opinion, view or judgement as to what is right and wrong. What I would say until you have stood face to face with someone like the guy I have just met, we will continue to believe the hype and moral panic that surrounds gang culture. Yes they are menacing individuals that have done all sorts of stuff. The truth is the solution for changing them will not be found in more incarceration, biased media coverage, or ignoring their existence. Gangs are a complex social phenomenon that requires more than just rhetorical posturing to sort it out. I don't have the solution, but what I did learn today, it starts with dialogue. But first you have to gain access. That access was created by Ted. The sad fact remains there are many guys like Ted, who don't get paid, supported, and validated for what they do. Yet he saves as many lives as any paramedic or surgeon. After 12 hours on the road Ted says he will drop me home. Suddenly five White police officers arresting a young black women forces Ted to stop, pull over, take out a video camera and record what they're doing. Ted archives stuff that happens on the streets as he wants to make a documentary on the abuses that take place on a regular basis. Low and behold it is taking place opposite Little Melvin's shop front. We stop off and talk with Little Melvin for about an hour before making our way home. I am thoroughly exhausted and take several hours to re-ground myself. What a day.

Undertaking this type of work in such difficult environments is seldom explored by filmmakers, as they are not full of tension and screen excitement. Inner city Baltimore introduced me to many layers of the criminal justice system; criminals who have desisted from a life of crime, but have themselves become victims of crime. Attempts to leave the gang, beating the court case by informing on others, and community justice in the form of revenge creates more victims. The difference here was that these individuals have no sympathy from society or the community, no free healthcare, or any clear future. Their lives are ruled by fear, governed by the code of the streets, and have little pathway to a new life. The prospect of having no money for living, healthcare, food, or personal items as a consequence of being involved in crime may leave society safer and the community feeling that justice has prevailed. However, the prospect of having absolutely nothing erodes any notion of pride and motivation to return to a life of law-abiding activity. This position results in forcing individuals back into the 'corners' as a way of surviving and restoring lost pride and status. In my view, I could not help but wonder what would have happened if black filmmakers were given the green light to create a series like *The Wire*. Again, progressive criminologists who are languishing on peer view waiting lists, may want to consider being advisors on TV shows such as *The Wire* or, better still, create criminologically grounded dramas for both the film and TV industry.

Postscript from a frustrated black writer

Having spent many years writing spec scripts, doing commissions I did not want to do, and trying to shot blast my way into the so-called mainstream market, I occasionally forget that it is okay to write stories that reflect my thoughts, dreams, and vision of the world. It was meeting many African-American screenwriters, theatre producers, writers, and academics in Baltimore that convinced me that there is still room for creative, commercial, strong, potent, and powerful ideas, with a diversity of black characters; black characters that fall in love, do things naturally, and have interesting three-dimensional lives. I had landed in an environment that was knee deep in successful, independent, self-motivated, and innovative individuals, who are moving away from the permission-seeking industry that renders many black aspirations redundant. I was reminded that too many of us have been so defined by the very same industry we attack, combined with other people's perceptions of what we are, that we have lost a sense of our creative identity. The fact remains that as both an academic and writer I still face the ordeal of being placed within the confines of other people's narratives, and spend many hours of creative energy reacting and responding to an agenda that makes assumptions that cannot be justified. As I landed back in the United Kingdom, I went back to my many rejection letters, old outlines, treatments, step scripts, and countless other pieces of finished and unfinished work. I started to read them again. What I realized was that I had good stories, but because I had grown up with a mindset that was damaged by rejection, I had forgotten that my job was to tell and write my stories, and not complain when they were never made. However, the drawback is that the industry sees black-led anything as biased and lacking in either context or relevance for wider British consumption. My stories usually do not fit the remit of many production companies or producers, or are not seen as 'fashionable'. I also reflected on the many Caribbean market scenes, churches, parental disciplining, urban battles, and so on – the array of characters, plots, twists and turns, adventure stories, killer dialogue, etc, that many of us have forgotten in the pursuit of the elusive blockbuster. As I look around British TV I am bombarded with so-called classical culture – Shakespeare, Charles Dickens, the Bronte Sisters, Thomas Hardy, and so on. This landscape all too often excludes people of colour and makes no apology for doing so. When does a white writer ever apologize for not having black people in their stories? And yet how many times am I told to be all inclusive in the name of Britishness? As white writers and academics have a right to reflect their perspective on life, so do I. It is like an invisible story in front of my face, and I, at times cannot see it. Our stories are all around us; they are in our family secrets – devious relatives, history, mythology, and folklore.

Show, don't tell

However, the question I must therefore ask sometimes is not what stories do I want to tell, but who do I want to tell them to? In selecting the stories I want to tell, I must ask myself yet another question: why can I not tell a story about the black contribution to British politics (for example, William Davidson in the Cato Street conspiracy) or write a documentary on the contribution of black writers like Chester Himes, Richard Wright, Walter Mosley, among others to the crime fiction genre? Making headway through the cultural industries landscape is bad enough and, without a clear, focused, and strategic approach in occupying the market place, a lot of black creative ideas are destined to stay at home with the piles of ideas languishing on shelves and occupying space within cupboards. There are critics who will see the need for greater autonomy for black talent as wrong, divisive, and in opposition to the colour-blind remit that does not see race as necessary within the genre of visual storytelling. But surely, in order to be equal, one must first have a sense of inclusion and belonging?

The prefix syndrome

As a writer who has written for all mediums, I have always desired to translate and adapt my own ideas into gripping pieces of TV and film drama that will hook the nation and get people talking. As a lover of crime dramas, I also enjoy the twists, turns, and general suspense as the plots unfold. However, I am dismayed at how those same crime dramas have a paucity of stories and themes that reflect the complexity of crime in society, combined with an absence of a diverse representations of characters seen on our screens. Whether the focus is on anti-social behaviour, serial murder, white-collar crime, or prison sentences, we have become a nation that watches, criticizes, and advocates a range of solutions to crime in society, but seldom do we explore the deeper context that might provide a new lens through which audiences may develop the tools to undertake detailed analysis of the problem of the way crime is constructed, viewed, and understood.

Reflection

Although film and TV formats offer the prospect of new, improved, and more nuanced portrayals of black criminality, it is the films of white filmmakers that ultimately have the leverage and power to continue to tell and own the cinematic retelling of black criminality. In spite of a vast history of black filmmaking, black-led projects are still relegated to the margins, even when those black filmmakers, male and female, tell good stories. Maybe it could be that black filmmakers, by turning the light on the structural determinants within our society, will move the conversations beyond super heroes, noir villians, and caricatures. The glue that binds most black art is music. The next chapter aims to explore a creative area for criminologists, students, and practitioners to consider, when investigating the role of music within the fields of rehabilitation, desistance, and probation type work as a whole. I have extensively used black music as a tool for rehabilitative work for over four decades – producing concerts, albums, musical theatre, as well as using the lyrical content within music when conducting prison forums to explore the messages conveyed. Black music in itself moves way beyond its commercial value and provides an outlet for the diverse range of experiences that at times are ignored within mainstream academic study. To embrace black music, means to embrace the culture and the people that produce it. It also confronts all of us with the politics and history that shapes the experiences that are communicated by the music itself. Both the sociological and criminological imaginations express the need to grapple with notions of history and culture, which would suggest that a black criminological imagination is an ideal home from which to explore the sociology of black music.

Provocation

How would you approach using black film in both teaching and learning when exploring pertinent issues in relation to black criminology?

6

Strange Fruit: Black Music (Re)presenting the Race and Crime

Chapter summary

This chapter aims to explore how the lived experiences of black offenders can at times be better understood by looking at the role that black music plays in their lives. I further argue that black music offers a safe space from which both to process and examine notions of positive black self-concept for black offenders. Black music can reveal messages, insights, and perspectives that illuminate the connection to, and relationship with, the structural elements that have disproportionately criminalized, incarcerated, and executed many black people.

Black music and me

As a lover of blues, jazz, reggae, and so many other genres of black music, I have similarly used the lyrical content of great songs to immerse myself in the highs and lows of black life, while the polyphonic manifestation of black music has influenced and impacted my understanding of black people, their criminality, and proximity to the criminal justice system, ranging from the power of reggae as folk music, jazz and blues as a rallying cry for civil and human rights issues, through to the uncompromising and defiant stance of hip-hop, UK grime, drill, and trap music. Black music has always illuminated my connection to, and relationship with, the structural determinants that have disproportionately criminalized, incarcerated, and executed, many black people. Whether I am listening to the music of Miles Davis underscoring a noir movie, being pinned to my seat by Public Enemy's powerful rendition of 'Fight the Power' in Spike Lee's movie *Do the Right Thing,* crying to the powerful words of acapella group Sweet Honey in the Rock, or nodding my head to the latest hip-hop, reggae, or grime track, black music has always been the glue that binds my personal understanding of my black experience. Important here is that the past cannot be divorced from the future when it comes to black music, which is inextricably linked to a culture that praises ancestors, chants, sings, laments, and expresses itself through the combination of words and music. Important here is to pay tribute to the durability of the black musical tradition that has survived slavery, emerged unscathed through colonialism, kept the civil rights movement going, and fueled the momentum for many of the black political movements we see today. I would go so far as to say that black music has provided much needed healing for a community whose history is far from bringing respite from the oppressive forces in society out to destroy the glue that binds those same communities who are constantly under siege from racialized oppression.

Black arts movements and music

All my life I have experienced the omission of my own historical presence regarding music emerging from people of African descent that to this day remains largely hidden, unless for the expediency of white corporations that tend to profit from the social commentary of hip-hop, the raw anger of drill, trap, and grime, alongside the hugely money-spinning exploitation of the reggae, Afro-Beat, and R & B industries. Even with the advent of recorded music, the black contribution was relegated to a sphere referred to as 'race records'. The term 'race records' was birthed in 1922 by Okeh Records (US) in reference to niche marketing of music aimed at African-Americans between the 1920s and 1940s. Race records were primarily musical genres such as blues, jazz, gospel, and comedy. During that time, few black musical artists were marketed to white audiences as the cost of buying music limited the consumption of produced music to African-Americans. Although black culture has greatly influenced culture as a whole, it was the expression of politics through music that charted the civil rights transition through to the black power movement and beyond. Music provided the conduit from which the experiences of those movements were mediated and enabled the average person in the community to listen to, and engage with, the events that were taking place at the time. As someone growing up in the 1960s, 1970s, and 1980s, I can attest that it was my exposure to jazz, blues, gospel, funk, soul, and reggae, that not only shaped my consciousness, but informed me about what was going on around me, as so-called mainstream society excluded such insights. In light of the nature of historical black oppression, the diversity of modes and forms of music has never provided a singular narrative from which the community itself can be unified. This in itself at times has been misrepresented as a division within the black community. The sound of revolutionary politics in the 1960s was expressed with artists who identified with the struggles and lent their voices to the cause. Similarly, other artists would recognize the need to provide escape and healing, and equally responded to the call. What is clear is that black artists and musicians are a vital part of any liberation struggle. So from where does the connection to criminal justice systems emerge?

Survival

Unnever et al (2019) suggest that whites purposefully construct a racially stratified society that oppresses black people, expressed through musical genres connected to black cultural production. Narrative criminology offers a similar rationale in the way it explores the stories of crime, minus the racialized constructs associated with black criminology. Presser and Sandberg (2015) argue that narrative criminology explores the storied bases of a variety of harms, and also consider the narratives with which actors resist patterns of harm. Narrative criminology in its orientation could offer a conduit for black music, where the stories presented through the music could reveal some evident truths about black people's investment in crime alongside the opposite to differential racialization. Presser and Sandberg conclude that narrative criminology cannot limit itself to the text of narratives, but must also include ways to understand what is 'not said' in narratives. Narrative criminologists should not only analyse stories, but also try to reconstruct them critically – in a way that resists domination and promotes social justice. Cashmore (1997) too argues that while we may enjoy a black culture in all of its saleable forms, we must remind ourselves of the misanthropic opportunities that brought it to our ears and eyes. In black culture we find a history of American violence, oppression, and racism that provokes reflection without spurring us into action. Amiri Baraka (aka Leroi Jones) (1963), writing in *Blues People*, recognized that the emotional limitations slavery enforced were monstrous; the weight of bondage makes it impossible for a slave to experience the many alternatives into which the shabbiest of free (white) men can project themselves. Kitwana (2002) also sees hip-hop music, no matter how widely accepted in the mainstream, as a voice for the voiceless.

Identity stripping

Goffman (1959) suggested that when prisoners are placed in a 'total institution' such as a prison, the barrier between the inmate and the wider world marks the first attack on notions of self. For Goffman, 'total institutions create and sustain a particular type of tension between the home world and the institutional world and use this persistent tension as strategic leverage in the management of men' (1959: 23). The participants in my research expressed a strong need to articulate a 'sense of their blackness' that they felt was rendered invisible during their time at HMP Grendon. This sense of blackness, they felt at times, was negatively pathologized. The sense of a 'loss of identity' featured heavily in the way black men in Grendon felt disempowered and oppressed. Du Bois (1938: 8) cites 'double consciousness' as a causal factor of black men's poor self-concept based on the impact of living in a racist society: 'one ever feels his two-ness, an American, a negro, two souls, two thoughts, two un-reconciled strivings two warring ideals in one body.' Having a sense of 'cultural invisibility' can compound this process. Ellison (1947) cites invisibility as a conscious act by white people designed to render black self-concept obsolete. Franklin (2004) also sees this deficit as a form of extreme social exclusion that he refers to as 'the invisibility syndrome', which severely limits black men's self-actualization. Black prisoners said they experience a similar invisibility in many areas of the prison regime: food provision (lack of cultural foods), reading material (black literature), staffing (little diversity) and little or no sense of being a culturally diverse community (small numbers of black men). As one prisoner at Grendon, 'C' told me:

C: It's hard, very up and down. You are judged straight away, for your colour and me for my size, for the way you talk, for the way you act. I feel that they don't really understand where I'm coming from and a lot of them don't really care either. If I'm honest I don't really know who I am. They are trying to make us like them, they're not letting me still be black, they're not letting me still have my culture, and they're trying to take that away from me.

'C' locates his current situation in Grendon as having his racial and cultural identity eroded, over which he has no control. Being in a minority situation is something that white staff and white prisoners may have very little understanding of or sympathy for. This state of affairs caused many of the interviewees to suppress their cultural and racialized identities, forcing them underground, combined with a built-up resentment and inner tension at the privileged position of white officers rendering those same identities subordinate:

Y: I've been here for three years and what I am aware of is this is a majority white male prison or white people prison. There is a minority of black or ethnic inmates here and there is a lack of understanding of us because there is not enough ethnics or blacks … they don't understand me, I've got to lower my lingua, I've got to lower the way I speak, the way I socialize.

'Y' highlights how the lack of validation of their racialized and cultural identities sets up a level of distrust that can, and does, create barriers to meaningful relationships with officers and other prisoners. Solorzano and Yosso (2002) argue that racism 'distorts and silences the experiences of people of colour'. This situation could explain why black men retreat, stay in the confines of the black community, and do not want to defend their racial existence (Spence, 2010):

P: You'll get a group of black guys walking on the yard and they're automatically labelled as, 'ah look at them they're back into their gang culture behaviour, loud, walking with a bit of a swagger and so forth and so forth'. You get a number of white people walking in their group but it's not an issue, when they do it.

The construction of 'racialized prison masculinities' at times generates stereotypical, negative, assumptions in some prison staff that can restrict the development of a positive self-concept for black men in Grendon. Listening to their life stories, it appears that although black men find being at Grendon beneficial in looking at and addressing their offending behaviour, they nevertheless experience identity difficulties through being minority members of the community. This leads to feelings of isolation and powerlessness combined with a sense that their cultural identity is insufficiently recognized. For black men who have been labelled and stereotyped, there is a need for them to create a new template for living. Counter-narratives from black men in Grendon would, as Zamudo et al (2011) suggest:

• challenge dominant social and cultural assumptions regarding black men's ability to name their own reality;

- utilize interdisciplinary methods of historical and contemporary analysis to articulate the linkages between societal inequalities and give voice to the experiences of black men in prison; and
- develop counter-discourses through storytelling, narratives, chronicles, biographies, etc, that draw on the real lived experiences of black men in relation to desistance.

A prison regime that does not see, acknowledge, or understand the impact of race and processes of racialization on black men will only serve to perpetuate the difficulties that some black men experience. The narratives of black men in Grendon laid the foundation not only for improving the regime but also for providing a culturally competent lens through which to do so. Interestingly, all of those I interviewed cited black music as the real therapeutic tool that enabled them to transform their lives. Without devaluing the therapeutic intervention, they were in a position to distinguish the difference between addressing cognitively their offending behaviours from the need to preserve their cultural and psychic well-being by remaining connected to their music.

Black music and criminology

If the previous chapters are the cogs that drive the engine of black life, then it is black music that is the oil that keeps it running. It is my contention that black music could support 'critical pedagogy' in the study of the racialization of crime. Critical pedagogy is a philosophy of education and social movement that developed and applied concepts from critical theory and related traditions to the field of education and the study of culture. Advocates of critical pedagogy reject the idea that knowledge is ever politically neutral and argue that teaching is an inherently political act, whether the teacher acknowledges that or not. The African captives transported across the Atlantic underwent a far-reaching and remarkable psychological transformation. The African-American generation of the 1950s and 1960s took the songs and hymns of our ancestors into the marches, jail cells, and mass meetings, and fashioned a faith of a movement that reinforced the African drum, chant, and music in an undisguised and transforming symphony of protest and revolution. At every turn, circumstances, dominant pathologies, events, and experiences all combined to ensure that black youngsters' experiences were markedly different and decidedly fractious, compared to those of their white counterparts. Jamaican music has always been genuine folk music but its story is seldom presented as a whole story. Rap is about freedom of speech and has become a battleground upon which an intolerant and powerful minority, most of whom happen to be white, has attempted to force its values against a disenfranchised and largely powerless minority, most of whom happen to be black. From the bowels of Bow in east London, the voice of a generation emerged, blinking furiously under the glare of capitalism. It was angry, loud, unapologetic, and innately provocative and fiercely independent. Questions of identity and rap music speak to an intimate and dynamic relationship, a relationship that is symbiotic. Identity impacts lyrical content and lyrical content helps to crystalize aspects of identity that might otherwise have remained hidden.

The past speaks

Robinson (1919) wrote eloquently about the importance of music for offenders, demonstrating the foundation of what continues to be a polarized debate between prison reformers and the punishment lobby:

> Poetry, painting, sculpture, have never existed for themselves alone, or even for the few who were equipped with the elements of artistic appreciation. But the art most universal in its appeal, because it is the spontaneous self-expression of even the most elemental of human-kind, is music. Music as the art essentially of self-expression, and not of representation, has been at work as a tremendous social factor ever since man began to have self-awareness, and his driving human urge toward self-expression found vent in sound, which is not less native rhythmic impulse finally tempered to pleasant intervals. But the question of the social utility of music is a vital theme for social theorizer and social worker alike. Of course, there are still extant among us penologists of the old school who insist that prisoners are merely happier for the influence of music in prison life, not morally better. Other equally practical criminologists say frankly that music, especially individual singing, seems to favour moral health. But all criminologists, whether practical or theoretical, must assent to the common-sense dictum that men are better for being even temporarily happier. On this simple fact as a basis, reformers of aesthetic trend have built various and wonderful theories, though doubtless most of them have strayed so far afield that they have quite forgotten their self-evident starting point. Nearly all of these theories sum

up in the statement that the criminal is out of tune with human harmony. Moreover, he is so repressed by prison discipline, and so used to the inhibition of native thoughts and impulses, that only a surrender, of his whole being to rhythmic freedom of thought and emotion can set him to be aware of himself as an integral unit. Through music he is again brought into harmony with the universal emotions of sympathy and pleasure. But one proviso must be made, the music must be well chosen. One has only to try the effect of music of the right kind on a band of unruly children or on a mob of excited people to recognize its efficacy as a social harmonizer. In fact, music demands the first necessity for social harmony – silence. It excites the first necessity also for moral readjustment – introspection. Folk-songs, then, since they spring from life, have a moral tonic quality not possible to the elaborate oratorio or to the artistic symphony. Moreover, singing the folk music has more moral value than merely listening to it. Music to be a weapon for the social reformer must, then, be psychological music, not mere artistic music. (1919: xx)

Robinson's views are as relevant now as they were back then. However, when you factor in racism in the criminal justice system, you can see why her words have gone unheeded. I now want to turn my attention to a groundbreaking musical project with young offenders that I was involved with called 'Colours'.

Colours

In 2012 I was asked to head up a music project called Colours, a programme that centred on 'Young People, Criminal Justice, and Music' commissioned by Lippy People, an organization based in Leeds, whose remit was 'to make a difference within our communities by collaborating to provide 'voice, influence and restorative justice' opportunities for people who feel marginalized, disenfranchised or ignored using collaborative filmmaking to achieve this aim.' The project sought to engage young offenders to represent themselves in the manner they intended by fully involving them in the production processes throughout. Traditionally in the criminal justice system, the voice of the offender is seldom heard. We wanted to capture a narrative through creative writing workshops and a documentary music video leading to practitioners gaining a better insight into the minds of young people, which will inform how they engage with them. To do so the following aims were established:

- understand the role of street and prison culture on the cognitive behavioural patterns of young offenders;
- help practitioners engage better with young people and have a greater understanding of the importance of their culture, language, and reference points;
- develop stronger intergenerational connections between prison officers and the prisons as a basis of improved prison management security and resettlement issues;
- challenge young offenders decision-making processes in a supported environment;
- start a process of change within young people.

The starting point was to get young people to explore how they themselves felt and saw key issues in their lives, specifically around guns, gangs, and knife crime. The workshops ranged over a couple of hours to a couple of days. A topic or issue that young people wanted to explore was selected using poetry, hip-hop, and grime, etc. The following pieces are examples of what young people produced.

Jail

> I feel lost
> I just can't think right
> Disrespect to my family
> Trapped in this bad place
> Deprived of my childhood
> Alone in my head
> Wound up all the time
> Sometimes I get sad
> Thoughts in my mind
> Ashamed by my crime
> Misunderstood all the time

(Written by 'D')

Here 'D' reflected on his time in jail. Prior to our arrival, 'D' was withdrawn, did not communicate with his peers, and expressed himself through violence. However, in using music 'D' found his voice and expressed his experiences, discharging his internal distress.

Jail

You're gonna face a loss
In the deep end you can't swim
You don't wanna get put in a box where you can't think
Yutes show disrespect
Guns are empowering dem
You don't wanna be trapped in a jail where you shower with men
No freedom so you're feeling deprived
You're feeling alone and not feeling alive
Wound up in a gang where you bang hammers
The roads are sad cos now we kill over colours of bandannas
Now it's a shame cos you're trapped in this gang ting
Now you're doing life for a misunderstanding

(Written by 'J')

'J' clearly articulates his experiences prior to coming to jail. At the age of 16 'J' was convicted of murder, and wanted to send a message out to his generation. Again, a young man like 'J', at the peak of his youth, lost his freedom. It was the power of music that enabled him to find the confidence to speak his truth. Important here is that much can be gained by deploying music in this way. The important point is that both 'D' and 'J' were young black men who talked of their frustration about how the absence of black music had an adverse effect on their lives while incarcerated. In my experience of running music projects in prisons over many years, I have observed how music has given many silent young black men a platform. Contrary to popular belief, not every young person who languishes in jail espouses anti-social behaviour. They desire to share their stories of poverty, violence, the code of the streets, and its relation to their criminality. Important here is that their stories, painful and as ugly as they are at times, offer researchers insights and understanding that can compliment the traditional data-gathering approaches used in our inquiries.

Case Example: David

During the same time, I undertook a similar residency with a group of black male offenders using the same approach. The following is a case study of David, at the time a young black man, who was sentenced to life at the age of 17. Here is what he had to say about that experience:

I was adopted and knew both my adoptive father who raised me and my father (the one who brought me into this world). I feel that I must describe both relationships. I have a good relationship with my adoptive father but feel we have become unintentionally more distant as I have grown up. When I was younger we used to go places and do things together but I don't recall having any significant father and son discussions. By that I mean father moulding his son as a child into a man. The relationship I have with my biological father is barely existent. On the occasional times that we do meet he tries to lecture me. I find it hard that under the circumstances he still feels that he has a right to take on that role. Even though I wouldn't say we have either a good or bad relationship. I feel that there is some kind of animosity when we're together. I can tell that like myself sometimes when we talk we're not comfortable. Creatively and through my music I believe I can show youngsters with talent that it's a must to express the gifts we have. As we never stop learning and I know that I personally need to mature more in certain aspects. I don't believe I'd be an all round role model. When I come around to raising my own children, I think I'll be in more of a position to be a good role model, especially if I achieve all the goals I've set for myself before then.

Unfortunately, David's involvement in crime resulted in him serving a lengthy jail sentence. It was on account of me overhearing him perform to his friends in jail that I stumbled on his true gift as a talented rap artist, who also produced his own music. What follows is an example of some of his work.

Another View – 'G'Rock

My self portrait ... irate 'N' confused
Chances abused ... mindstate misused
For years your views ... land on hard ears
Now at night yer voice ... echoes in my eyes
Shed tears ... if my life's been written
Then the authors cold ... how many chapters
Before my stories told ... lay the book to rest

No more beats in my chest ... yer warm lips on mine
But that's wasted breath ... I've done left – this world
No more fight inside ... it's kinda strange how yer life
'N' mine coincide ... glide through dese times in a
Millennium rush ... da ghetto thugz buss ... causin' 'N'
makin' ships sink ... an eclipse got anorak people
Tickled pink ... To be continued ...

Again, here is what David had to say about his life during his time in jail:

> Being in prison has taught me to deal with anger completely
> differently to how I have done in the past. I used to act on
> impulse which has got me into more problems, but while in
> Prison I've faced so many no win situations with 'authorities'
> that I've learnt to channel my anger into a positive instead of
> a negative tendency to bottle up a lot of anger, depression,
> and regret. This causes me to breakdown at times and cry in
> private. I feel that crying does relieve us of a little stress and
> I know that at times I do feel a need to cry. We all have a
> certain amount of stress inside us and we've all been through
> different things leaving mental scars and inner pain. I've
> already stated that I bottle up a lot of my inner pain and try to
> avoid sharing the way I really feel with people. I don't think
> I actually know how to deal with my inner pain, so it gets
> bottled up with everything else I keep inside. My advice to
> the younger generation would be to keep their own mind.
> Don't allow anyone to mislead them and whatever goals they
> set for themselves stay focussed and determined to achieve
> them. Remember, it's easier for someone to discourage you
> from doing something positive than it is for them to do
> something for themselves, which is why they mock.

Over a period of many years, spanning three decades, David began to
make sense of his life, experienced much growth and transformation
where his music was a constant companion in his life. Within the
poignant lyric below, 'Thoughts', David resents a redemptive narrative,
with some clear recommendations for the next generation.

Thoughts ...

Why avoid difficult tasks?
No joys come without a struggle

It's easy to criticize
but!!!!!!!!!!!!!!!!!!!!!!
how does it feel to be criticized?
Within each boy lays the foundation of a man
The same way we mould plasticine figures
We mould our lives
If you don't show your son the way
He'll find his own
We grow inside a woman for 9 months
We then live for a period of time
Being fed from a woman's breast
As a boy we cry for mum (Woman)
Then grow into men and disrespect our women!!!!!!!
No man has a right to put his hand on a woman
The people at the top of the mountain had to climb up!!!!!
Why do we feel bad when someone else makes it?
We'd rather not try than fail
Although we are judged wrongly we fall into the trap
It's easy to be sheep but what's it like to lead?
Don't walk away wishing you'd voiced your opinion,
Voice it!
There could be 200 racists and 50 Black men in a hall
And the violence would probably be Black on Black – Why?
I should respect your mother like I respect my own
Crying doesn't make you any less of a man
Why argue when we can discuss?
Why shout when we can talk?
Why so much hate and so little love?
Instead of helping you climb I wait for you to fall
To gain knowledge it must be sought

By using music, David was able to reclaim a new identity, while at the same time improving his self-concept. McAdams (1988) maintains that individuals like David, who can make sense of their lives in the form of 'life story' or 'self-narrative, may be better able to transcend their 'at risk status' and be reintegrated into the community and ultimately desist. Maruna and Roy (2006) also suggest that life changes, such as desistance from crime, may be shaped by a process of 'knifing off' – the means by which individuals are thought to change their lives by severing themselves from detrimental environments. The challenge of returning ex-prisoners is much more than their physical relocation into their home community. Instead, the challenge that reintegrating former prisoners like David into the community from which they came is more psychological. Paternoster and Bushbay (2009) likewise argue that before individuals are willing to give up their working identity as a law-breaker, an individual must begin to perceive this identity as unsatisfying, thus weakening their commitment to it. They further argue that those wishing to quit crime are more likely to be successful at desistance if they are embedded in social networks that not only support their new identities and tastes but also isolate them from those who would oppose them quitting crime or induce them to continue in their criminal ways. By providing encouragement, opportunities, and structures through which they can function as full members of the community, returning prisoners like David can become positive contributors to community life.

Reflection

This chapter lays no scientific claim regarding the transformative power of black music as a tool for rehabilitation. However, in my experience, which is no less valid, black music could play a greater role in unearthing, preserving, and presenting stories of black criminality that can support other approaches that fail to connect to the lived reality of black offenders. For many black offenders, black music is more than just entertainment. It embodies a series of truths and hidden histories that both contest and challenge the narrative that has painted black criminality as something that has no justification or rationale. To those critics I would suggest you listen, study, and understand black music. When looking at black people and their offending, whose stories do we privilege? That one question has led me to develop both my practice and academic work, which argues for the acknowledgement and validation of the stories that black offenders themselves tell of their own understandings and insights into their criminality, which must also enable them to both 'narrate' and 'interpret' their own reality by bringing coherence to their 'real-life' stories (McAdams, 1988). The word 'myth' comes from the Greek word 'mythos', meaning a word or story. Storytelling, therefore, is an ancient art, where people would tell stories passed down through the generations by word of mouth. Stories bind people together and allow each individual to better comprehend their place in the world. It is my view that acquiring passed-on wisdom and knowledge can provide a space for black offenders to tell their own stories as both the experts and knowers of lived reality in relation to their criminality.

Provocation

What role do black artists and the wider black community play in introducing black music as a component that could give valuable insights into the lived reality surrounding black criminality?

7

Of Mules and Men: Oral Storytelling and the Racialization of Crime

Chapter summary

This chapter aims to look at the tradition of black storytelling in relation to black people and the retelling of their experiences. Folktales, storytelling, and oral history are not unique to black culture. However, the importance of locating the black storytelling tradition within the racialization of crime and criminal justice can provide an importance legacy for future generations about the past ways that academics and historians have fallen short when looking at the racialization of crime and criminal justice.

Black stories matter

This chapter contains many examples of the stories I used in my rehabilitative work with black offenders. I urge you to take the stories, adapt them and use them within your own context. For many black people, a history of subjugation and racial oppression has placed a massive strain on acquiring a sense of authenticity in relation to understanding their place in the world.

Using stories over many years to inspire, motivate, and uplift many individuals in the community, or in a prison, I would see how stories enabled them to work through problems using the 'story wisdom' that was imparted. McAdams (1988: vi) writes that, 'we understand people in terms of their life stories, the dynamic narrative that we each create to make sense of the past and orient us towards the future'. McAdams further suggests that, 'stories represent critical scene and turning points in our lives', and that the life story 'is a joint product of person and environment'. Therefore, stories represent something fundamental about the way we see life and how we learn to navigate key turning points in our own 'life story'. In areas where individuals are disaffected, socially excluded, and marginalized it is especially important. As damaged individuals they cannot possibly reach their full potential, if they do not know how much potential they have. Therefore, by engaging in *storytelling* and *story making* as a generative activity using storytelling as a method of communication and connection in the black community may strengthen intergenerational ties relationships. Erikson (1950) explained that generativity is the interest in establishing and guiding the next generation. Storytelling, therefore, creates possibilities for both personal reflection and self-evaluation, leading to self-growth. This position could have significant benefit for black offenders regarding what Agnew (2006) terms 'storylines'. Storylines, as Agnew argues, begin with some event that is out of the ordinary, and this event temporarily alters the individual's characteristics, interactions, and/or settings for interaction in ways that increase the likelihood of crime. Agnew sees storylines as having a clear beginning, a middle, and an end. Storylines begin with a particular event; where something happen to the individual. This event represents a deviation from the routine aspects of the individual's life that momentarily affects the characteristics of the individual, the individual's interactions with others, and/or the settings encountered by the individual in ways that increase the likelihood of crime. The storyline ends when some event restores the individual's level of strain, social control, social learning for crime, opportunities for crime, and individual characteristics to their prior levels. In essence, Agnew is using much the same as narrative criminology that explores the ways that stories of crime influence crime and other harms. However, the tradition of storytelling goes back centuries and did not start with criminology. There is a tradition of black storytelling that can be deployed in both the retelling and reimagining of behaviours, attitudes and insights regarding the racialization of crime. This next section is dedicated to showcasing some of my own use of stories as a generative practice. My role within the process is not to act as an academic or researcher, but as storyteller. The storytelling session begins with a grounding exercise where I tell the story, followed by active discussion with the participants, who draw their own conclusions and apply it to some aspect of their lives that may need clarifying or changing. Many black people I have worked with have sought guidance from elders and credible messengers, as a way of receiving wisdom in a safe and supportive way. The following stories are for you as the reader to use as you see fit.

Aesop's Fables

Aesop's Fables are credited to Aesop, a slave and storyteller believed to have lived in ancient Greece between 620 and 560 BC. 'Fables' are short stories that illustrate a particular moral and teach a lesson. The theme and characters are often humorous and entertaining. The characters in fables are usually animals that act and talk just like people while retaining their animal traits. The fables are all very short. The objective is to use each story as a moral lesson in life. Below is Aesop's fable, 'City of Lies':

> There was a young man, traveling in the desert, met a woman standing alone and terribly depressed.
> 'Who are you?' He inquired of her.
> 'My name is Truth,' she replied.
> 'And for what cause,' he asked, 'have you left the city to dwell alone here in the wilderness?'
> 'Because in earlier times, falsehood was with few, but is now with all men,' she answered.

Below is my adaptation entitled 'Truth':

> I hadn't felt this bad in a very long time. The nine shootings in a Charleston church left me physically sick and empty inside. The news of nine dead black bodies being cut down by a twisted young white man five thousand miles away cut deep. This tsunami of pain overpowered me like the scent of rotten perfume. So much was the intensity of the deafening silence of lingering death that night my head hurt. This was no work of fiction; but what unfolded was a real Greek tragedy where the outcome went way beyond the actual physical victims of 'white rage'. I tried to imagine the terror and fear on the faces of those who survived this vicious attack, but somehow I couldn't get beyond the look of the self-styled assassin Dylann Roof staring at me through the TV, brandishing a gun, draped in the confederate flag. There are so many times when I've heard people pass comments about not dwelling too much in the past, in spite of history frequently being

used to keep the conquests of others alive and well in my sub-conscious. The amalgamation of the Confederate flag, South Carolina, and Church, reminded me that this history was real. I reflected on Sidney Poitier's 'In the Heat of the Night', Alex Haley's 'Roots', and numerous other movies I'd watched depicting the brutalities of slavery and segregation. Was it a case of art imitating life, or life imitating art? The veins in my temple throbbed with the kind of intensity reserved for a migraine. I had to get out of the house, which felt claustrophobic and eerie. Walking through the cold streets I was oblivious to my surroundings and had no awareness of how fast or slow I was going. I just needed to shake off the darkness that had now descended on me like a dense fog. I headed towards the midnight chimes coming from the large clock tower beside the park. The park was a place where I could always find solace in troubled times. It was my sanctuary where I could escape from the noise of the treadmill I'd grown used to. We used to call it 'scary park' growing up on account of its neglect over the years which gave it the appearance of playing a starring role in a horror movie. It didn't really have a lot of public facilities and was more of a cluster of old trees, decaying paths, a dried up lake, all surrounded by unkempt greenery. In some respects the decrepit state of scary park felt like a metaphor for the community I lived in. I used to watch couples in love, loads of dog walkers, combined with an assortment of individuals who used to tend it with some good old tender loving care. I remember as a child going on picnics with my parents and listening to live music in the bandstand on Sundays. Somehow the memories of those moments were drowned out by the sound of an owl hooting and the whistle of the midnight wind. There was a certain sadness knowing that the technological revolution had now pushed many back into their own little spaces, where the 'moral panic' that surrounds open spaces forces parents to abandon spaces like scary park. The community I loved was now full of selfishness and was full of post-modernists who lived for now, didn't care about the past, and had very little need to move beyond the confines of the suburbs. I'd lost track of the time and just fell into the moment. Amongst the darkness and silence a figure in the distance caught my attention. At first I thought it was a statue but as it was moving I realized that there were at least two of us on the planet that didn't find scary park, scary. I approached with caution as I didn't want to cause alarm. As I drew closer the figure stopped, turned around and looked directly at me. A woman, dressed in a large yellow cloak, a long flowing green dress, and an African headdress with an air looked completely out of place. Her lingering stare caused me made me feel awkward and uneasy.

'Are you lost?' I called out.

'No' she replied in a firm but soft tone.

'Are you okay?' I inquired.

'Fine' she replied 'and you?' she concluded.

'I'm taking some fresh air' I continued.

'From what?' she asked.

'Things' I mumbled.

'Things like what?' she pressed.

'You heard about the shootings in Charleston?'

'Yes' she replied.

I don't know what it was but her answer made me smile. Knowing someone else had heard about the shootings felt like an opening for a much needed conversation. The more I looked at her I couldn't help but wonder who she was. There was an air of mystery and sophistication that was striking.

'So how do you feel about the shootings?' I asked.

'You ask a lot of questions?' she replied.

'I'm sorry. I'm just curious that's all' I went on.

A smile opened up on the woman's face which reassured me.

'What's your name?' she asked.

'Roy' I replied 'Yours?' I asked.

'Truth' she replied.

'Truth?' I asked.

'Is my name that unusual?' she continued.

I blanked with all the subtlety of a school child forgetting the answer to a maths question when asked by the teacher.

'I'm sorry, but I've never met anyone called Truth before?'

'I was given this name by those who came before' she replied.

'You mean your parents?'

She went quiet and said nothing for what appeared to be a long time.

'At a time when the world was in darkness and troubled I was sent to walk amongst those who were suffering' she continued.

'Sent? I'm confused. Who sent you?' I interrupted.

After a lengthy silence she walked off at speed. For a brief while I stood fixed to the spot wondering what to do. However curiosity got the better of me so I ran after her.

'I'm sorry' I apologized clumsily. 'I didn't mean to come across the way I did. Can we start again?' I asked hoping to get a reprieve.

Truth stood there and looked straight at me with a piercing stare that was uncomfortable.

'Are you a social worker?' I bumbled.

'What is a social worker?' Truth asked.

I blanked, followed by an uncomfortable silence.

'What do you do?' Truth asked.

'I thought I was an advocate' I replied.

'Advocate?'

'I help the community and assist people to better their lives' I continued.

'It sounds good'.

'Is it?' I replied with my head bowed.

'Why are you crying' Truth asked.

'I'm tired of being tired' I cried.

'Tired?'

'I talk to young people all the time about not being violent and then I see a young white guy shooting 9 people dead in a church' I finished.

Truth lifted my head and stared hard into my face that was now full of tears.

'I was there with Frederick Douglass, Harriet Tubman, and Sojourner Truth. I was there with Martin Luther King and Malcolm X, I was with Nelson Mandela, and Ghandi, I walked with them in Selma, occupied the streets of Ferguson and Baltimore and still no one listens. Human life can be wretched when falsehood is honoured above truth' said Truth.

The site of a fox took me off guard. I turned around and Truth was gone. I stood silently for a while before heading home trying to figure out what had just happened.

The importance of this story is it is used as a prompt within community settings when looking at 'truth' and its relationship with our current live realities. The story when told also provides a context from which to explore creative ideas that provide offenders with whom I work with a sense of agency, where their interpretation of the story is given a platform free from judgement, as all their views matter.

Trickster stories

One of my favourite experiences as a storyteller is presenting 'trickster' tales. Almost all mythology has a trickster hero of some kind, be it the Native American Coyote, African-American Brer Rabbit, African and Caribbean Anancy. There is a special property in the trickster: he always breaks in, just as the unconscious does, to trip up the rational situation. He is both a fool and someone who is beyond the system. In short, the trickster:

- is always an outsider among animals or humans, whose outrageous actions, remind us of our own human weaknesses;
- always lives in the wilds, but regularly invades the human community causing mayhem and chaos;
- disturbs the peaceful order of things;
- openly competes with anything human, animal, or magical.

At the start of each story everything is harmonious but, by the end of the story, chaos ensues. Ultimately order is restored, but not without a price being paid. The trickster in storytelling terms is a great character when looking at morals, ethics, and values. The characteristics of trickster stories follow a pattern of progression. The trickster forms a *contract* with friends, family, or community, which leads to a *deception*, using cunning or *trickery* where the trickster violates the contract. Then comes the *dissolution* of the contract and everything it stands for. Invariably the trickster always gets away, not unscathed, but usually unpunished. It is this situation that creates ideal material for further discussion. These deceptions of the trickster can have quite grave consequences on individuals, communities, and society as a whole.

Brer Rabbit and Brer Fox clash (US)

Brer Rabbit was a quick thinker and played pranks on other people making them very angry. Now Brer Rabbit and Brer Fox were like a couple of little children. Both of them were always after one another, playing tricks making sure no-one got a minute's peace. Brer Fox did all he could to catch Brer Rabbit, and Brer Rabbit did all he could to keep him from being caught. One day, when Brer Rabbit and Brer Fox were working in a field, the sun became really hot, and Brer Rabbit got tired. But he didn't let on, because he feared the rest of them would call him lazy. So he screamed out that he got a thorn stuck in his hand. Then skipped off and hunted for a cool place to rest. After a while, he came across a well with a bucket hanging in it.

'That looks cool, I think I'll just get in there and take a nap.' Brer Rabbit said. And with that, in he jumped, and he no sooner fixed himself in the bucket than the bucket began to go down. As soon as the bucket hit the water Brer Rabbit started to relax, glad that he'd got out of doing work. Meanwhile Brer Fox had watched Brer Rabbit walk off. He knew Brer Rabbit was up to no good and followed him. Brer Fox crept up a little closer to the well, and listened. But he didn't hear any noise, so he got even closer. Yet he still didn't hear anything. All this time Brer Rabbit was mighty near to being scared out of his skin, and he was afraid to move because the bucket might keel over and spill him out into the water. Brer Fox called out, 'Brer Rabbit! What are you doing down there?'

'Who? Me? Oh, I'm just fishing, Brer Fox,' said Brer Rabbit, 'I just told myself that I'd sort of surprise you all with a mess of fishes for dinner, so here I am, and there are lots of fishes'.

'Are many of them down there, Brer Rabbit?' said Brer Fox.

'Lots of them, Brer Fox; scores and scores of them. The water is alive with them. Come down and help me haul them in, Brer Fox,' said Brer Rabbit.

'How am I going to get down, Brer Rabbit?'

'Jump into the bucket, Brer Fox. It'll fetch you down all safe and sound.' Brer Rabbit sounded so convincing that Brer Fox jumped in the bucket. As he went down, his weight pulled Brer Rabbit up. When they passed one another at the halfway point, Brer Rabbit sang out, 'Good-bye, Brer Fox, take care of your clothes, for this is the way the world goes; some go up and some go down; you'll get to the bottom all safe and sound.' When Brer Rabbit got out, he galloped off for home, and when he got there, he flung both hands over his face and laughed. As for Brer Fox, he eventually got out of the well and even more determined to get his own back on Brer Rabbit.

Again the trickster was used in many of my rites of passage sessions with violent offenders. There were many occasions where black offenders I worked with did not trust therapy, white researchers, or any authority figures. Frequently, they would complain about built-up frustration that at times led to violence. Trickster stories would be used to explore alternative ways to reduce the tendency for violence and resolve conflict.

Uncle 'P' and Marcus stories

While visiting relatives in Jamaica in 1989 I met my very wise granduncle, Uncle 'P'. As I sat and listened to him tell stories, it struck me that not only was he entertaining, but his ability to educate me with his wisdom was truly a memorable experience. It is for this reason I decided to create two characters Uncle 'P' and Marcus, loosely based on my granduncle and me. Marcus is a young 10-year-old boy, who faces problems in his life and goes to Uncle 'P' to assist him in understanding them.

Whose loyalty?

'Should we follow other people when they tell us what to do?' asked Marcus.

'Why should you want to follow other people?' Uncle 'P' replied.

'Some bullies at school want me to join their group' replied Marcus nervously.

'What did you tell them?' asked Uncle 'P'.

'I said no, but they told me if I didn't join them, I'd be in a lot of trouble', Marcus responded in a shaky voice.

'They're only trying to test your loyalty' said Uncle 'P' in a reassuring voice.

'Loyalty, what's that?' a confused Marcus asked.

'Loyalty means they want you to be part of their group and no one else's' replied Uncle P.

'But I'm scared, so what do I do?' asked Marcus in a shaky voice.

'Pull up the story stool and sit down' instructed Uncle 'P'.

Marcus sat down on the old stool eagerly waiting to hear another great story. Uncle 'P' leaned forward and the wise teacher then began the story ...

... A wise man called a meeting with his three sons.

'As you can see I am growing very old. Soon I will no longer be able to look after myself,' he said. The brothers looked at their father and nodded in agreement.

'The time has come for you to go out into the world to see if you can provide for me in my old age'. Again the three brothers agreed. The very next morning they set out on their journey and came to a large river. The eldest brother spoke to the two younger brothers.

'I think that it is time that we go our separate ways. In one year's time we shall all come back to meet again at this exact spot'. The youngest brother went to the left. The middle brother went to the right. Whilst the older brother went straight ahead. So the brothers parted. At the end of the year they all met again at the same place on the bank of the river.

'What did you bring back from your travels?' the older brother asked the youngest.

'The only thing of true value that I found was a mirror. It is a magic mirror. Whosoever looks into this mirror can see every place in the world, no matter how far away it is,' replied the youngest brother.

'I have a pair of sandals. They too are magical. Whosoever puts them on can walk to any place in the world with only one step,' answered the second brother.

'I have found a small calabash filled with medicines', said the oldest brother.

At this point the brothers decided to look into the mirror to see how their father was doing. The three brothers became very sad, for they saw that their father had died while they were gone, and had already been buried.

'We must return home immediately to see if there is anything that we can do', said the oldest brother. Without a moment's hesitation, the second brother pulled out the pair of magical sandals. Together the three brothers put their feet into the sandals, and in one step they were beside their father's grave. Now the oldest brother took out his small calabash filled with medicine and poured it on the grave.

No sooner had the medicine landed on the grave than the father rose up revived and well. He greeted them happily. The three brothers told their father about their journey and the things they had discovered. Which one of the brothers served their father the best?

Equally as important is to use stories to explore morals and values. The previous story has been used extensively in my work, designed to enable prisoners to openly discuss the moral contained within the story – an important rehabilitative tool.

Issue-based storytelling: the consequences of knife crime

When tackling issues such as knife crime, violence, gangs, and the consequences of dangerous actions, I have found telling stories is a far more effective tool in enabling young people involved in serious youth violence to open up and discuss their behaviours. I wrote this story over 30 years ago, but it has proved every bit as successful now as it was back then.

Omar's misadventure

At school Omar had been bullied so many times because he didn't fit in. Although Omar never found it a problem, others did and made him pay for it. Those who bullied Omar pressurized him to be a follower, a clone, and tried to control his life. They didn't want Omar to be an individual with his own ideas, thoughts, and feelings. Instead, they wanted Omar to be part of their crew. With each day at school came torment, verbal abuse, and physical attacks. Omar tried to defend himself, but felt powerless as he couldn't fight back.

The other kids at school laughed at Omar and called him weak, useless, rubbish, and good for nothing. It got so bad that Omar started to believe that he was no good. No one listened, no one helped, and no one understood what Omar was going through. Omar was alone, depressed, and becoming angry. Then one day he snapped coz he'd had enough. He wasn't going to take it anymore. Omar decided that it was time to stop the bullying once and for all. At home Omar started to have all sorts of crazy thoughts about what he could do to those who bullied him.

Anger stood in the corner of Omar's bedroom encouraging Omar to get even with the perpetrators and convincing him to act on his feelings. Omar listened intently to anger as he received instructions on what to do. Omar was now poised and ready to go into battle. As Omar was about to leave to go to school *Stupidity* called him back into his bedroom, and told him not to leave without a weapon. Omar placed *a small knife* in his pocket and gave *Stupidity* a hug before leaving. Omar turned the corner and was met by *Foolishness* who gave him some last minute instructions as well as introducing him to three new people *Nervousness, Anxiety, and Fear* who all talked and joked with Omar. In the distance *Bravery and Reason* called out to Omar, but *Stupidity* stepped in and pushed them away. *Stupidity* ran up behind Omar and stayed close behind to monitor the situation.

On the bus Omar was joined by *Temper,* eager to help him in his quest to deal with those who had bullied him. *Temper* passed on a few brief pieces of valuable information to Omar before leaving as quickly as he'd arrived. In the distance *Love* watched helplessly, as *Death* danced up and down on the spot, knowing he might meet Omar at any moment.

Omar reached the school playground and scanned around. His eyes focused on those who had bullied him. Omar started to feel weird, and was met by *Confusion*, who introduced himself to Omar before giving him a reassuring pat on the back. Those who bullied Omar gathered together and headed towards him. Omar started shaking whilst *the knife* in his pocket started to speak to him; saying how wonderful things would be now they are going to be working together. Omar felt comforted, as *Badness* had given him a few handy hints on dealing with the situation.

Omar's heart now pumped faster and faster and faster! *The knife* gave Omar some last minute instructions and told him exactly what to do. The bullies surrounded Omar and then started pushing him around. *Bravery* and *Foolishness* came to Omar's aid and tried to help him, but they too started to fight with each other and left Omar on his own. *The knife* then screamed at Omar and cursed him for taking so long. *The knife* told Omar that it was time and urged him to act quickly.

Cousins *Hostility* and *Rage* appeared on the scene and came to the rescue. They stood either side of Omar and whispered in his ears. Omar lost control and plunged the knife into one of the perpetrator's chests. A loud scream followed by a drop on the floor made everyone scatter. The perpetrator stopped breathing, whilst Omar ran off. Omar paused for a while to catch his breath when he was met by *Revenge* who came over and congratulated him on completing his mission. It was over! No more bullying … no more torment … no more pressure for Omar anymore. The problem was solved.

Omar was 15 then … he's 19 now, 4 years into a life sentence. Omar now has three new friends; *Loneliness, Depression, and Suicide.* They love Omar and share the same cell with him, 24–7. They talked to him every minute of every day.

Like true friends they're always there for him, never leaving his side, whilst *Death* sits quietly and reads the latest bestseller entitled *'Come to me: The art of persuasion though violence'.* Death was in no hurry.

Omar … A WASTED LIFE!!!!!!!!!!!!

Letter writing as stories

As a child, I wrote to Santa Claus as my mother created the magic of Christmas that centred on creating a wish list, dreams, and desires that were fuelled by my fertile imagination. In my teenage years I similarly discovered the art of writing letters to accompany my early stirrings regarding 'social injustice' where I would write letters of complaint and opposition to injustice. Bounding into my 30s I continued to write letters to secure employment, make inquiries, alongside keeping in touch with friends and family. For me, writing letters meant using a pen to express my love of words. There is something in the wording, phrasing, and expression that, to this day, I find particularly satisfying. It is also important for me to note that at times of emotional distress I write letters to myself, as a way of reframing negative thoughts. Little did I know that all of this work was my apprenticeship for my greatest letter writing endeavour. In 1985, I found myself working in the US (Boston, Massachusetts) with a community activist called Linda Thurston, who gave me a rallying call regarding liberating the voices and narratives of serving prisoners in the US through the power of letter writing. Fast forward to 2020, and I reflect on the sheer volume of letters I have written to incarcerated individuals for over four decades. My archive of letters spans dozens of men and women; sharing their testimonies and lived experiences in relation to the criminal justice system. Two people stand out in particular: Nyati Bolt and Al Cunningham. I was introduced to Nyati by Linda, who gave me his details in Angola prison (Louisiana). Throughout the years of incarceration until his release, we have been in constant contact, now as friends. Al, languishes on death row (San Quentin, California) and has been communicating with me for over 25 years. Both men have insights into everything, from politics to general life issues, that have challenged many of my own values and beliefs. Whereas an email can be impersonal, lack substance, and be sent to many people at the same time, a letter is bespoke, personal, and incredibly intimate.

Letter from Al (2002)

Dear Martin

Chained and shackled, I was taken away from my family, away from my freedom, shipped, stripped, stacked and packed into small cells of a jail where my true test of mental survival would be tested and my endurance for sadistic torture would be put under experimentation. I would soon come to realize what a hard and constant struggle it would be to daily maintain my sanity and mental & physical survival under such conditions. I am daily stripped of all Clothing and put on display. Paraded in front of· an audience of observers whose eyes penetrate with their stares of 'Wonderment, lust and hatred, while their thoughts are forming within their minds of their next forms of tortures. I am cheated of my rights as a human being, cheated of proper legal representation, cheated of and denied all forms of justice, and segregated. This time can be used however each individual chooses. You can use it constructively or like a glass of water, just sit and allow dust to set on top, to become stagnant in a vegetative state. The cell is not large enough to stretch your arms in. My cell is 4 feet in width, 10 feet in length, and 8 feet in height. It has a cold steel slab for a bunk. I can lay on my bunk with my shoulder against one wall and reach out and touch the other wall without straightening my arm. The food slot is directly in front of my bunk, so I can lie down in the bunk and reach up and accept the food being slide in through it. I have TV sitting on two cardboard boxes at the end of the bunk in front of the toilet.

Both sink and toilet are made of stainless steel and both are at the end of the cell. Above them recently have been placed in our cells, is a steel shelf with four compartments. I have a typewriter sitting on two cardboard boxes in the centre of the cell. I can sit in the middle of the cell in front of the typewriter and reach everything in the cell. Other than that there is nothing else which can best describe this cell other than the words 'Isolation' and 'monstrosity'. We are disrespected, denied, rejected, degraded, discriminated against, stripped naked at any given time and place. Personal belongings are searched and thrown all into a pile, stepped on, and totally tossed about the cell so as to create a negative reaction from the inmate. Our mails are scanned, searched, rejected, and sometimes even the officers will write some of the correspondence if they think they can get over, or discourage someone from writing to us. The fear is always there just around each corner. It is a world of violence, hostility, stagnation, and retrogression into adolescence. It is a time of educating oneself on surviving on little or nothing and developing shameful habits. So such practices continue in full confidence of the public's disbelief and unconcern for such persons as prisoners. Having endured all this, day after day, month after month, and year after year, I still manage to mentally and physically survive. I still rise to face each day with hope, obscuring my inner strength and savouring what personal inner accomplishments I may have made, achieved, consummated by unseeing eyes. There are many nights I've laid awake, listening to the sounds of the night, wishing I were someplace else. Listening to the sounds of car horns, babies crying, construction workers making irritable noises, and above all, experiencing the freedom I so desperately crave. The night so. Still, I can almost hear the dreams of others as they lie sleeping on their steel cots dreaming their dreams, as the night moves on. The hours seem to past so slowly at times, but then, before you realise it, it is the dawning of a new day. Once again, I will be forced to listen to the obnoxious yells and screams of others as they hold their nonsense conversations. Some talking loud because they want to be noticed by others, they feel a need to impress others, they suffer from a deep feeling of lack of self-worth. Others, talking to cover up their fears, and gain strength from the rest.

Then there are those who talk and make noise simply to hear the sound of their own voices. I'm tempted to think I am in some sort of insane asylum instead of a prison. Grown men, acting like undisciplined children and babies. I wonder how many others are thinking in the same way I am forced to listen to these disturbing individuals. Then I also wonder how many times have I had to catch myself from acting in such immature behaviour? How many times have I had to prevent myself from cheapening my character and self-control? How many times have I had to refrain from depreciating my intelligence? It can become so easy to demean one's self when there is little to seldom any positiveness emitted within this element of walls and bars. No encouragement, no inspiration, and seemingly, no hope.

In closed institutions such as prisons, letter writing becomes the basis for many incarcerated individuals to find an outlet for their feelings, which are supressed based on the deprivation of liberty. There is richness of expression, an honesty that underpins the stories of pain and loss, which is combined with knowing that this shared dialogue is both a shared and co-produced relationship. Letters capture important moments in a prisoner's life and are driven by multiple stories that form the basis of a wider narrative. Al's letters have informed me about life on death row in a way that research at times fails to capture. The future for research of black men's experiences of re-entry and desistance should, therefore, involve listening and hearing the 'narrative' of black men themselves. This 'narrative' must address itself to the process of both social and political change for men in relation to criminal justice policies that affect them. As modern living is at times fraught with complex, difficult, and confusing challenges, there is a need to re-establish a series of guiding principles and truths by which we can reframe our lives. Storytelling provides the ideal conduit for handed-down and passed-on wisdom that is both sacred and spiritual. The fundamental need to explore who we are, why we are, and where we are, requires a strong foundation from which ideas can be presented and accessed in honest, truthful, appropriate, and relevant ways. At all times, the messages presented should be informed and grounded within a context designed to uplift, guide, and enable the receiver of this wisdom to move to a new point of self-awareness, personal transformation, and holistic understanding. Stories are about individual and collective memory, defining meaning, and finding purpose. McAdams (1988) suggests 'that we understand people in terms of their life stories, the dynamic narrative that we each create to make sense of the past and orient us towards the future' (p. vi). McAdams further suggests 'that stories represents critical scene and turning points in our lives', and that the life story 'is a joint product of person and environment'. Therefore, stories represent something fundamental about the way we see life and how we learn to navigate key turning points in our own 'life story'. Spence (2010) advocates that space where one does not have to defend who one is should be enshrined within the overall ethos of any institution that prides itself on good race relations. Socio-historical marginalization and psychological invisibility also present difficulties for some black men, while mono-cultural and Eurocentric notions of therapeutic intervention can at times make it difficult for black men to develop a strong culturally appropriate identity and sense of self. Developing a stronger black self-concept must involve the re-organization of damaging beliefs and values through storytelling. Prison regimes and community support services that do not see, acknowledge, or understand the impact of race and processes of racialization on black men will only serve to perpetuate the difficulties that some black people experience.

Reflection

Every community member should participate and submerge themselves in stories as a way of processing the world around them. Stories open up our world, boost the imagination and give us self-knowledge. Stories also bind people together and allow each individual to better comprehend their place in the world. Returning to the past to gather ancient wisdom as a guide and a template to reframe, reinterpret, and reinvent our lives can enable all of us to transcend our difficulties and be guided to a new place. By adapting ancient wisdom into a new storytelling paradigm, the possibilities for new personal growth are endless. The use of myths, folklore, parables, trickster stories, and so on should act as a complimentary part of our lives, as important as food, shelter, and love. Going back to retrieve our stories is not about nostalgia, nor is it something that is just for the very young, it is about a journey of self-discovery and personal transformation. Storytelling can assist in making one's journey in life, when transitions occur, such as ill health, aging, marriage, births, etc. Over many years I discovered that storytelling and story making can be used to harness our personal potential, while at the same time increasing the possibilities for growth and change on many different levels. It is my view that storytelling and story making can assist all of us in reclaiming a new identity and consciousness. In areas where individuals are disaffected, socially excluded, and marginalized it is especially important. I have always used my work to enable, empower, and inspire those same individuals who not only have potential to change, but also possess the ability to transform the lives of those around them. As damaged individuals they cannot possibly reach their full potential, if they do not know how much potential they have. Therefore, by engaging in storytelling and story making as a 'rite of passage' it may be possible to transform individuals and, in turn, whole communities. Black stereotypes are driven by a narrative where African enslavement and racial hierarchies that the tipping point for European colonialism. In a world where people take selfies, flood social media platforms with self-generated images, and are generally driven to obsessive heights to attain standards of beauty that for many people are not attainable, it is important to assess how this plays out in terms of the self-concept of black offenders. In schools we see a sparse representation of black people who have shaped society. Newspapers seldom highlight black attainment through visual means. Indeed a constant frustration of my wife is not seeing herself presented in affirming ways in adverts. Where black people are seen, they are seen protesting, in crime stories, in bit parts in soap operas, or in any other areas society sees fit to present screen-saving tokens to satisfy a hunger than never wanes. However, black visual art – from the traditions emerging from indigenous art, urban forms such as graffiti, and more contemporary styles – is an important tool that can be utilized within criminology when looking at notions of identity, culture, and representation for black offenders.

Provocation

Whose stories should be privileged when looking at the racialization of crime and criminal justice?

Seeing the Story: Visual Art and the Racialization of Crime

Chapter summary

This chapter examines a little-known area of black arts in relation to the so-called mainstream arts landscape, that of black visual art. In spite of their historical presence in the United Kingdom, black people still push towards greater representation and racial parity as expressed through the movements discussed in this book. Indigenous people worldwide are still struggling to gain full and equal status within countries that were colonized, while black people are still viewed as outsiders. Derogatory and negative depictions of the black visual presence are actively promoted in advertising and, when they are sensitively drawn, they are seldom driven by black people themselves.

The need to reframe who we are

Webster (2007) argues that black offenders, who end up in the criminal justice system and prison, are disproportionately represented compared to their numbers in the population. Patel and Tyrer (2011) express the view that when race enters the 'othering' process, particularly within the context of crime and deviancy, it is important to consider the roots of racially charged concepts that disproportionately target minority groups such as black people. Similarly, Gabbidon and Taylor-Greene (2012) argue that the disenfranchisement of black people involved in crime is ideologically driven as a way of bolstering the carceral estate. Tonry (2011) proposes that these 'racial disparities' are unjustifiable and are more about the maintenance of political dominance over blacks. Tonry concludes by arguing that the visualization of black people through the media, film, and TV has created a culture that views black people as criminals and as being predisposed to anti-social behaviour. Marable (1995) also suggests that inequality for black people involved in crime is based on black male stereotypes that white society imposes via institutions, and says the wider social structure generates the type of inequality that produces subordination for black people within the criminal justice system. If the picture painted of black criminality as aggressive, nihilistic, and purely criminal enterprise embeds itself in the consciousness of society and constructs racialized typographies of people as 'criminal', what are the consequences for the way black offenders achieve parity? Valdes et al (2002) argue that academics, activists, and artists must enable the subordinated person through a critical examination of black offenders' own understandings so that their redemptive aspirations can be appropriately identified and understood. A major outlet for all offenders in UK prisons is 'Koestler Arts', one of the UK's best-known prison arts charity, established in 1962 by Arthur Koestler.

Koestler Arts

The charity awards, exhibits, and in many cases sells artworks made by prisoners. The use of art in this way is justified by the following aims:

- to help prisoners, secure patients, and detainees to lead more positive lives by motivating them to participate and achieve in the arts;
- to increase public awareness and understanding of arts by offenders, secure patients, and detainees.

The Koestler Awards attract over 7,000 entries a year, across more than 50 different art forms. These include creative writing, poetry, music, painting, drawing, mixed media, photography, ceramics, and craft. Exhibitions showcase the talent and variety of Koestler Awards entries each year, including our national exhibitions at London's famous Southbank Centre. So art is clearly important within criminal justice. However, at a time of the proliferation of right-wing populism that is at times supported by the press and wider media, I fear that the visualization of black imagery is at the mercy of corporations, which, through slick branding and marketing, can seriously present a reductionist pathology of the victims of white supremacy.

Dismay

West (1993) argues that the black diaspora's invisibility and namelessness can be understood as the condition of relative lack of power to represent themselves to themselves and others as complex human beings, and thereby to contest the bombardment of negative, degrading stereotypes put forward by white supremacist ideologies. An interrogation of black visual art in relation to the racialization of crime and criminal justice therefore becomes important here. A clear example of the power of visual art was in the murals dedicated to George Floyd. His death was signaled to the world, not just in newspapers and TV broadcasts, but in the visual representation of artists who wanted to memorialize the image of an innocent man who died at the hands of the police. During the late 1960s, the Black Panther Party artist Emory Douglas created visual messages for black people struggling against severe oppression. Douglas' work metaphorically armed black people with imagery that enabled them to defend themselves against daily injustices. Douglas' intrepid and carefully constructed images were compelling, but conversely, they motivated law makers and law enforcement officers to disrupt the organization aggressively. Decades after mainstream media vilified Douglas' work, new generations celebrate its prescient activism and bold aesthetics. Douglas created visual mythology that merged fluidly with the ideas of Afrofuturism, which would develop years later as an expression of imagined liberated black futures. African creative arts arrived on the slave ships while traditional visual African art was referred to as 'primitive' by Western artists. The mistake made here is that much traditional African art was conceptual not representational or realistic. Another element of African art is in its functionality, in relation to everyday life. So if the framing of the production of art is flawed, how then does the visual representation of the black aesthetic stand a chance in a world dominated by white aesthetic judgements and values? How then do black offenders generate positive visual imagery, if the memories emblazed in their consciousness is one of pain, hurt and loss?

The Black Art Group

In 1982, the Black Art Group was the name chosen by a group of four influential conceptual artists, painters, sculptors, and installation artists based in the United Kingdom: Keith Piper, Marlene Smith, Eddie Chambers, and Donald Rodney, who were based in the Midlands.

The group were all from the British African-Caribbean community and exhibited in a number of group exhibitions in both small and prestigious galleries throughout the country. Their work was noted for its boldly political stance, producing dynamic conceptual art that offered a series of inventive critiques on the state of inter-communal, class, and gender relations in the United Kingdom. They were influenced by a variety of artistic currents, including ideas associated with the US Black Arts Movement. Eddie Chambers has argued that, despite their undoubted creativity and social relevance, the group suffered from the general lack of serious critical attention given to black artists by the British arts media. Nevertheless, their enthusiasm and commitment to making art relevant to everyday life ensured that they were a strong influence on the later generation of black British artists that included young black artists such as Chris Ofili and Steve McQueen, both of whom went on to win Turner Prizes, while maintaining a clear political element to their work. What did emerge from the initial impetus of this movement was the response of poets, dramatists, storytellers, dancers, and numerous others who, like our African-American cousins, were experiencing racism, denied access, and oppression on a large scale. Equally as important was the role played by the Rastafarian movement, reggae sound systems, carnivals, and numerous other artistic institutions that were complimentary components that made the overall thrust of the movement truly diverse across the whole UK black community.

Roll call

As the art scene is promoted as traditionally white, I want to give a shout out to those black artists who have generated impact even if much of their work has remained hidden. The list that follows is definitive, but a roll call of important figures for you to investigate further:

- *Frank Bowling*. Alongside other major figures – notably Ronald Moody, Aubrey Williams, and Uzo Egonu – Bowling was part of an influential group whose art came out of London in the decades following the end of the Second World War, and who set the stage for the further impact of black British art. Interestingly enough, Frank was given a knighthood in 2020. Yet his contribution to the so-called mainstream art establishment has been largely overlooked.
- *Chris Ofili*. The first black artist to win the Turner Prize, part of the Young British Artist movement in the 1990s.
- *Uzo Egonu*. Fuses Western and African styles drawing on the heritage of different cultural traditions to create something new.

- *Sonia Boyce.* Deals with themes of race and gender: a visual representation of her experiences being a black woman living and working in Britain.
- *Lubaina Himid.* An important figure in the emergence and development of black artists in Britain in the 1980s, and as a curator of black artists' exhibitions, both gender and non-gender specific.
- *Donald Rodney.* Instrumental in pushing for greater representation of black art in Britain. Sadly he passed away far too young.
- *Lynette Yiadom-Boakye.* Paints portraits, but her subjects are not real people: they are composites, made up from bits of real people and bits of photos taken from magazines and her imagination.
- *Keith Piper.* Along with his contemporary Donald Rodney (above), Piper made waves in the 1980s art scene.
- *Tam Joseph.* Resisted attempts to pigeonhole his work as being only about issues of race.
- *Winston Branch.* A largely abstract artist.
- *Vanley Burke.* Originally from Jamaica, now living in Birmingham, Burke has been described as 'the godfather of black British photography'. From humble beginnings, this black artist is renowned in the world of photography.

Many contemporary black artists have continued to use art to contest, confront, and challenge racist stereotypes, by exploring black embodiment within the production of their art. It is also true that during the 19th and 20th centuries, many black artists attached themselves politically to art movements designed to dismantle racism.

- *Robert Seldon Duncanson* (1821–72). Well-known for his landscape paintings.
- *Meta Vaux Warrick Fuller* (1877–1968). At the fore of the Harlem Renaissance and also known as a poet, painter and sculptor.
- *Augusta Savage* (1892–1962). Associated with the Harlem Renaissance, and committed herself to equal rights for African-Americans in the arts.
- *Joshua Johnson* (c 1763–c 1824). Known for his paintings of prominent Maryland residents.
- *Henry Ossawa Tanner* (1859–1937). The first African-American painter to gain international acclaim, he spent most of his adult life outside of America, mostly in Paris.
- *Jacob Lawrence* (1917–2000). Inspired and influenced by the bright colours of Harlem as well as by French art.

- *Kara Walker* (b 1969). Uses diverse mediums such as painting to filmmaking. Walker is best known for her silhouettes, made from black paper.
- *Kehinde Wiley* (b 1977). An America portrait painter described as highly naturalistic, his works revolve around the painting of black people.
- *Nastio Mosquito* (b 1981). His art uses performance, video, music and poetry.
- *Iona Rozeal Brown* (b 1966). Known for paintings influenced by printmaking and hip-hop.

The importance of the roll call was to draw attention to the fact that black people have contributed to the wider culture even if they have been ignored by so-called mainstream arts establishments Similarly, it is my experience working in criminal justice that a major amount of visual art is created and produced by black offenders, but is seldom seen or even heard of. In particular, I have worked with many long-term offenders and indeed those on death row, who all escape into the world of their visual imagination to deal with the trauma of the weight of an oppressive racialized history and criminal justice system. A traumatic event involves experiences that completely overtake our ability to cope with those experiences. Traumatizing events can take a serious emotional toll on our confidence and beliefs, even if the event did not cause physical damage. This can have a profound impact on our sense of self, resulting in negative effects in mind, body, soul, and spirit. Simply put, traumatic events are beyond a person's control. It is not the event that determines whether something is traumatic to someone, but the individual's experience of the event and the meaning they make of it. Because the traumatic experience was so terrible, it is normal for people to block the experience from their memory, or try to avoid any reminders of the trauma; this is how they survive. However, the consequences of these survival mechanisms are a lack of integration of the traumatic experience, such that it becomes the experience in a person's life, rather than one of many. The trauma becomes the organizing principle from which the person lives their life always trying to cope with and/or avoid the impact of the trauma. In my view creating visual stories as a tool for healing has always been a central component in creating space(s) for individuals and groups to speak safely to each other without judgement or fear of recrimination. Asante (1987) cites a move away from Euro-centric hegemonic knowledge into a grounded form of Afro-centricism that may start to bring some significant change within the current 'misplaced consciousness' of people of African descent. Oliver (1989) also sees

African-centred socialization as an interactive process that promotes values of love of self, via awareness of one's African cultural heritage as a conduit. Developing a stronger black self-concept must involve the reorganization of damaging beliefs and values. Visual art embedded into a black offender's rehabilitative process could offer a way forward as part of a wider push towards black visual arts as cultural therapy.

Visual art and desistance

Maruna and Immarigeon (2004:43) see desistance in criminological research as 'the termination point at which offending ceases'. More recent explanations highlight an expansion of insights and understandings within the discipline pointing to the complexity of factors that influence desistance and support self-agency in relation to understanding 'why and how former offenders avoid continued involvement in criminal behaviour'. However, within the theories of desistance there is a distinct lack of attention paid to black offenders. Connell (2003) criticizes those social scientists who fail to recognize diversity in their work and concedes the attention paid to race and culture is scant. Wilson (1994) argues that a young black man with no self-concept will be motivated by self-alienation, exhibit an ignorance of his ethnic heritage, engage in unbound hedonism, manifesting in deep insecurities, regarding his masculinities and masculine courage. Pinnock (1997), in his work with South African gangs, roots his rites of passage paradigm within a firm criminological framework, by contrasting prison as destructive rites of passage designed to trap and punish the perpetrator. Pinnock argues that rites of passage as part of a process of restoration provides liberation for the criminal as well as healing for the community that has been affected by destructive behaviours. One cannot develop notions of self-outside as a conduit for developing and delivering it. How then do black offenders, who have been both labelled and stereotyped, assume a healthy position in a society that systematically has relegated them and their aspirations to the margins of society, and create a new template for living? If black offenders cannot develop a positive self-concept it is questionable whether they can maintain a focus that will enable them to desist from crime. Creating a new paradigm that will enable black men to consider new choices that could divert them away from crime is essential for society as a whole. Engaging black men in processes such as art making that will liberate them from the pain of social neglect and denied access could play a significant role in taking them from a social position of being seen as a liability into the realms of being acknowledged as an asset to themselves, their families, and, in turn, the community. A need, therefore, to reframe criminology itself could provide a new paradigm that would place black men and desistance within a relevant and appropriate context. Over the three decades of my work as a workshop facilitator, I have used visual arts with community people and offenders that act as a safe and accessible form of 'therapeutic intervention', which could be drawing self-portraits, doodling, collage, crafting, or looking at art works.

Towards black visual arts as cultural therapy

Since the late 1960s, African-American psychologists have been examining the development of ethnic awareness as a culturally based empowerment process that reaffirms self-worth and enhances personal efficacy in black offenders. Services must seek to heal the whole person instead of addressing various symptoms as they arise. To increase the wellness and the health of black offenders means taking action to restructure the mental health system to be recovery-oriented, community-based, and to bring systemic transformational change to correct dysfunctional systems dynamics that will support emotional emancipation and healing for black offenders. There is the need to build more accepting, inclusive, and diverse organizations and communities in broad-based population efforts for prevention and early intervention of mental issues in people of African ancestry. Through the promotion of visual arts as a conduit for healing and reformation of the spirit, the black community, in my view, already has systems and networks in place that can assist the healing and support required by black offenders both in an out of prison. However, these systems need to be supported and funded for sustainability, continual outreach, and ongoing development of serving organizations and agencies. For services to complement their engagement with and delivery to black offenders, they must strive towards the development and creation of processes that are also 'culturally competent'. It is also my view that a visual arts model of cultural therapy for black offenders could inform and shape both criminal justice policy and practice, with offenders as a whole.

Reflection: towards a model of visual arts as cultural therapy

The model of visual arts therapy for black offenders would critically assess how this intersection enhances or impedes the psychic and cultural functioning of black offenders, in relation to their self-concept.

This position is based on a range of assumptions that require further investigation:

- Black offenders are disproportionally represented within the criminal justice and mental health systems.
- The historical distortion and negative portrayal of black people within society has resulted in significant response and adaptations as a consequence of living in a racialized context.
- To develop a positive 'self-concept' and 'psychological identity' requires a reorganization of one's self in relation to being black and an offender.
- To bring to the fore how race and racialization within the criminal justice system impedes or enhances the overall mental health and well-being of black offenders.
- To challenge traditional research and evaluation methods that fail to legitimize the social, historical, and political experiences that inform the way black offenders make sense of their own world.

Overall, this model would examine the interplay between psychology, culture, and visual arts as a way of understanding how the values and beliefs of black offenders are shaped by notions of 'racialization' within the criminal justice system. As much of a black offender's lived reality focuses on having to contend not just with the criminal justice process, but with the additional oppression of racialization within the wider criminal justice, the outcomes become more heavily context-dependent and driven. Denzin (2010: 6) suggests that, at the beginning of a new century, it is necessary to re-engage the promise of qualitative research as a 'radical democratic process'. As a process it focuses on the meanings that research participants give to their lived experiences via the narration of events that brings coherence to their own real lived concerns (McAdams, 1988). It is against this backdrop that 'data verbalization' was born. Data verbalization 'speaks the data'. It is my contention that 'data verbalization' can give researchers a unique and distinct platform from which to generate significant reach and impact, beyond the academy, conference, and peer-reviewed journals.

Provocation

How would you justify using black art to a diverse group of students as a way of understanding the lived experience of black people, their criminality, and racism, without letting bias get in the way?

Speaking Data and
Telling Stories

Chapter summary

The importance of breaking free from the peer review journal and conference circuit within academia requires the creation and production of criminological counter-narratives contesting some of the biased claims made by many white academics and scholars when disseminating research data centring on black criminality. This chapter envisions a way for research data to be seen, heard, and experienced using a frame of reference that is unapologetically black, creative, and accessible to the wider community. 'Data visualization' is a technique that is widely used in both academic and corporate circles to present data in visual formats to explore difficult concepts or identify emerging new patterns contained within statistical data.

Context

The narrative potential of presenting research data creatively should offer the possibility of restorying the past and reimagining the future. The importance of creating a more contemporary and culturally competent approach to research data dissemination then became critical. In recognizing that few scholars have attempted to actualize the intersection of research data and the spoken word beyond the academy, the context for this development was set. Research impact centres on the understanding that generating knowledge by conducting research should contribute, benefit, influence, and transform the environment, culture, as well as the the wider society. To do so requires developing innovative approaches to producing knowledge that work alongside disseminating research data/

findings using innovative and creative means. For most of my working life I have used creative approaches to my work – storytelling, poetry, theatre, and film in a variety of contexts and situations. However, the real challenge was to investigate how 'creative dissemination' of research data would stand up to scrutiny regarding issues concerning 'validity' and 'reliability'. To my delight I discovered 'bricolage research'. Bricolage research is a critical, multi-perspectival, multi-theoretical and multi-methodological approach to research inquiry. The French word 'bricoleur' describes a handyman/woman who makes use of the tools available to complete a task. Bricolage research in essence means unifying multiple qualitative research approaches. For progressive researchers using, a bricolage research approach creates an exciting new proposition. In October 2016 I was given a small development grant from Birmingham City University to develop the Data Verbalization Lab, an experimental space for individuals interested in using the data berbalization technique on their own research. For several weeks I ran the programme I had devised for a diverse group of participants, consisting of undergraduates, postgraduates, doctoral students, and community members. The resulting outputs resulted in the creation of data verbalization – spoken word pieces, theatre performances, creative podcasts, and screenplays. Excited by my discovery, I was also approached by a music producer who agreed to work in partnership with me to adapt some of my own research into a jazz hip-hop fusion. The result was the production of my debut data verbalization single called 'Silenced', which is currently available on various social media platforms.

Moving beyond boundaries

Research dissemination, whether it is a written or oral representation of our project findings, tends to happen at the end of a research project. It brings closure to a long process, where a hypothesis is either proved or disproved, or something amazing has emerged that may result in change, raised awareness, or simply feeding back. As many of us know, the modes of dissemination – such as the journal article or conference presentation – often restrict audiences to other academics and distance many researchers from seeing their research bound into practice and action. In my view it is time to envision a future project that requires *all* community members to actively be involved in creating a new frame of reference from which to begin the restoration of some of our most marginalized communities through 'liberatory' approaches to research dissemination. Akom (2008) argues that, as educators, we need to find numerous ways to build stronger agency within research participants and place them at the centre of their research – from data gathering, analysis, through to dissemination. During my doctoral studies I was given advice by prominent sociologist Howard Becker regarding using a creative approach when advocating around issues associated with criminal, social, and racial justice. He urged me to 'persuade' my critics, 'convince' the sceptics, 'empower' those I engage with, and to 'transform' the lives of oppressed, marginalized, and disaffected communities by using non-traditional approaches to critical inquiry and dissemination. This led me to start thinking about the role of praxis within research data dissemination. Brown and Strega (2005) express the view that there must be a willingness to explore the emancipatory possibilities of new approaches to research, even when these transgress the boundaries of traditional research and scholarship. It is my view that knowledge production is assessed based on legitimizing certain information generated by certain people in certain ways, which is accepted or can qualify as truth. If knowledge creation is separated from praxis, then how do we grasp the messy complexities of people's lives, especially the lives of those on the margins.

Praxis

Practice is often depicted as the act of doing something. It is usually contrasted to theory – abstract ideas about some thing or phenomenon. In this, theory tends to be put on a pedestal. From theory can be derived general principles (or rules). These in turn can be applied to the problems of practice. Theory is 'real' knowledge while practice is the application of that knowledge to solve problems. Praxis is an iterative, reflective approach to taking action. An individual engaged in praxis is well prepared to participate in collective actions: '*Praxis* is a commitment to human well-being, the search for truth, and respect for others. It is the action of people who are free, who are able to act for themselves' (Carr and Kemmis, 1986: 190). Freire (1970) argues that the oppressed unveil the world of oppression and, through the praxis, commit themselves to its transformation. In the second stage, in which the reality of oppression has already been transformed, this pedagogy ceases to belong to the oppressed and becomes a pedagogy of all people in the process of permanent liberation. Praxis, in its simplest construal, means theory plus action. It indicates life practice formed from both reflection and action. The self, striving to transform the world creatively according to an emerging vision based on its own values, actualizes itself as it actualizes its vision. Because individuals' actions always affect other people, praxis is inherently political. Praxis refers to a particular philosophy used to guide and conduct research. Like action researchers, those who engage in praxis-oriented research involve the community or group under study in the research process. However, praxis is distinct in that its explicit goal is to empower marginalized peoples and help them challenge their oppression. Engaging in praxis is not a path for the harried researcher interested only in quickly collecting and analysing data. Praxis-based research is a long process that involves establishing mutually beneficial relationships between the researcher and members of the community of study. Denzin (2010) argues that for 'subordinated voices' to be heard, they must be 'helped to speak'. Equally as important is the view of Bochner (2014: 315), who writes: 'Listening to different voices and trying to express your own, about trying to muster the courage to speak the unspoken even if it terrifies you'. Denzin further argues for 'performative social science' paradigms that provide some new answers to old problems.

Augusto Boal

Brazilian theatre director Augusto Boal was in sympathy with the oppressed and believed in 'theatre as praxis'. Boal also encouraged critical thought about social conditions using theatre as the conduit and developed the 'Theatre of the Oppressed' to great artistic and intellectual acclaim. Over the years, much of my own work in criminal justice, public health, and education has built on his creative and philosophical ideas, which has in turn informed the direction of my future work. Similar to Boal, I believe that those of us who are engaged in 'critical inquiry' should utilize 'performative approaches' when conducting research that is socially and culturally driven. This approach serves as a tool for both maximizing the potential of research that affects people's lives, alongside increasing the potential 'impact' of the research itself in relation to personal, community, and social transformation/change. Working as a researcher, I have observed how both 'quantitative' and 'qualitative' research reports tend to be disseminated mainly through traditional means – conferences, seminars, workshops, etc – where the format is quite predictable and, at times, some of the important messages, insights, and understandings can and do get 'lost in translation'. This, in my view, weakens the research as a whole, if the 'feedback-sharing' of the outcomes is relegated to mere 'sound bites' or 'small chunks of information' that raise awareness, but do not result in the implementation of important recommendations. For me, this state of affairs is troubling, especially when the demand of much contemporary research is to:

- make a difference;
- give value for money;
- be groundbreaking in its visoning, scope, and impact.

It is, therefore, my view that performing research offers researchers, practitioners, business organizations, third sector organizations, and policy makers an important opportunity to present research that can be experienced through observation, active participation, and interaction.

Data verbalization is the way to go

Data verbalization? A term I conceived after seeing the global impact and success of its quantitative cousin 'data visualization'. The need to generate a parallel and complimentary revolution around 'performance-driven research dissemination' for qualitative researchers is situated as part of a wider continuum regarding accessible methods associated with presenting challenging and complex research using creative methods such as data verbalization. I started with a blank canvas from which to extend the boundaries of research dissemination that would be appropriate for use in today's social media savvy world.

The inventory

On completion of the following inventory it is important for you to consider some of the ethical choices bound up in disseminating your research using data verbalization. Ethics are an essential part of the research process, as they set the boundaries between the researcher and the subjects of the inquiry. Similarly, data verbalization is ethically driven from a performance standpoint. I now turn to the process of adaptation.

Stage 1 – Finding a premise

Firstly, it is important to generate a premise from which to build your data verbalization story. A premise is the core theme or idea underpinning the article, usually located within the abstract. The process starts by selecting:

- a journal article;
- a research report;
- other data-driven source material.

Now I had identified the premise behind my data verbalization story, I could begin to identify those themes within my paper that connected themselves to the overall premise. A story premise works in much the same as undertaking a literature review that addresses itself to the research question. The premise is the guiding principle that forms the foundation of the data verbalization story. In essence, if the story you are telling works effectively, then the audience will understand the premise that underpins the narrative.

Stage 2 – Highlighting

Once you have your premise read your article many times over to internalize the story of the article. On becoming familiar with the overall narrative drive of the article, highlight key phrases/important words much the same as you would do when undertaking thematic analysis or grounded theory. On completion of this exercise, transfer the highlighted information to index cards and group them into categories. Structure your phrases and words into codes and categories by laying the cards out in front of you. By doing so you can begin to restructure the cards that build into a story. As academic journal articles are full of ideas that flow in a linear fashion, it is important in the adaptation you observe the rules of storytelling, by creating a story that has a clear beginning, middle, and end.

Stage 3 – Rhymes

Using rhyme is the most rewarding part of writing any lyric, but the most frustrating if it does not work. To write rhyme well takes practice. The careful use of the right word at the right time can make or break a piece of work. To avoid forced rhyming (rhyme made because you cannot find the right word to match another) use a dictionary, rhyming dictionary or thesaurus to assist you. As you now have a premise, a range of sentences/words, arranged themes, and a basic narrative structure, you can begin the task of generating rhymes to accompany the data verbalization story. This phase requires a significant amount of rewriting, resulting in many redrafts, until you have the final draft. It is vital that you create rhyming patterns that flow and are consistent.

Stage 4 – Studio recording

The following is a breakdown of how the process works.

- *Composition*: Working with a music producer means now relinquishing elements of the overall control of the process. Whereas at the beginning of the process you were the sole author of the piece, it now becomes part of a collaborative enterprise. This next phase of the process is about composing and producing music that moves the work from the page and eventually onto the stage.
- *Finding the premise:* The producer first listens to the adapted material minus any music. By doing so the producer can assess the required tone and cadence of the piece overall. This is then followed by the scoping of a range of musical ideas. At this stage, both the producer and I listen to the emotion, rhythm, movement, and timing that balances and complements the voice of the orator. Once both the producer and I are happy with the musical choices, it is time for the producer to work independently.
- *Sampling, chops, time stretching, grooves:* The production team then spend hours going through jazz/blues music, which is then used to sample the initial music track. Sampling is a process used in the music industry where a small amount of an already produced piece of music can be extracted to lay the foundation for other recorded tracks. The sampling equipment is a creative beat making with an acclaimed live sounds and sounds library.
- *Making the drum beat and patterns:* Almost every tune has a kick drumbeat, which defines its rhythm. Beats come in groups of four that are called bars. The first beat of every bar is usually stressed to make it distinguishable from the other three. The bars are in turn grouped into four and eight chunks called phrases. For example, a four-bar phrase has 16 beats. Phrases are of key importance when you which consists parts of intro and verses with phrase changes of an even number every 16 bars, where most normal tracks have an intro verse and chorus and consist of an even number of four-bar phrases with regular intervals that normally equal one or two eight-bar chunks.
- *Arranging the track:* The song structure usually uses drum kick, snare, clap, and piano chords sampled to create a hook for the track. This is then followed by inputting actual piano sounds to complement the musical phrase changes. The importance of this process is the working on the relationship between the words and music, to create a blended piece where one element does not dominate the other. In essence, the arrangement is a digital version of classical composition. It is the process that brings the finished track to life, emphasizing the nuances within both the linguistic and musical elements of the piece overall.

- *Voicing the track*: Before I can voice the track, I am sent a version to listen to, practice, and immerse myself fully in what the producer has created. Working in a recording studio requires me to develop the skills of microphone techniques associated with digital recording. The microphone is very sensitive and will pick up any sound. Hence there is the need to practise avoiding doing several major takes. I also learned that it is easier to use a computer from which to read my work, acting much the same as a tele prompter on TV. Holding paper to read your work can result in 'paper shake', which can be an inhibiting aspect of studio recording.
- *Mastering for release:* Mastering is the final stage before releasing the track, which is the final technical and complex music production process, within the confines of a very accurate studio environment (acoustically and in terms of reference grade, full spectrum high resolution monitoring). Its goals are sonic corrections though use of equalizers and dynamic control, enhancements, volume balancing, decision making relative to perceived volume, sequencing and spacing of tracks, final quality control now that the vocals are recorded. The next stage is to release the completed track on all media platforms.

Example: code switching

The following example emerged by taking some exploratory notes I had written that formed the basis of an article. By deconstructing the text, extracting the themes, and making them rhyme, the resulting outcome what what is now termed 'data verbalization'.

> Kenneth B. Clark said Dark Ghettos have invisible walls erected by a privileged White society
> Where those who have power, confine, constrain 'N' induce massive levels of Black anxiety
> Dark Ghettos are places of hope, despair, conflict, resilience, pain, vibrancy, 'N' apathy Courage, defeatism, cooperation, concern, where there is little direct support or sympathy
> Privileged White communities blind themselves to the marginalized 'N' the disconnected
> Meanwhile middle class Black people exchange Blackness for Whiteness, going undetected
> Hovering like a humming bird, emerging from Black shadows, behaving like they're rich

'N' the Black Bourgeoisie change sides, devise a new 'code' 'N' eventually they switch

Du Bois refers to this position as living in a state of racialized 'double consciousness'

Where some Black people move to a 'White' space, feeling now they can progress

E. Franklin Frazier said some middle class Black people live in a glossy world of make believe

As they want to leave their Black roots behind, coz they feel they can't 'move on' or achieve

Many don't like to be associated with the Ghetto by day but return back to it at night

'N' when the 'White' space rejects them, they ask themselves a question 'fight' or 'flight'?

This then causes pain when 'Black comfort seekers' are told to conform 'N' know their place

'N' like a pendulum they swing, between 'Ghetto Blackness' 'N' the privileged White space

Steele and Aronson see this psychological state referred to as a 'Stereotype Threat'

Where the assertion of their Blackness makes suburban house Negro's panic 'N' sweat

To avoid confirming a negative stereotype they cast off their 'Black 'N' Ghetto' masks

Redefine their identity, try to blend in, whilst performing the master's biased tasks

This internalization of 'inferiority anxiety' comes from the 'White space in their soul

Once the dice has been thrown, this retreat from ghetto Blackness, begins to take its toll

The transformation is complete as they transition from the 'Ghetto', into the 'White space'

Cut themselves off, exiting the Black zone where they vanish quietly without trace

Elijah Anderson says 'White spaces' create 'N' produce a level of partial racial integration

But Black occupation of the 'White space' requires a more detailed 'N' critical investigation

Although the White space supports some racial progress, the ghetto is still exclusively Black

Whilst the White space lets a few Negro's in, whilst the Ghetto continues under attack

In the White space Black people are absent, marginalized, not heard or seldom seen

In the White space, there can be no reggae beats, hip-hop, or the red, the gold, 'N' green

Now the White space demands Black people adjust their comfort level to one that is White

Whilst the fear of having a 'Black suburb' breeds fear about what it will bring up, or ignite

This cosmopolitan ideal paints a picture of 'separate but equal' White 'N' Black spaces

The White space imports some Blackness, whilst the ghetto comprises of mainly Black faces

Ghetto people approach the 'White space' with trepidation, caution, stealth, 'N' fear

Whilst coming to the ghetto for middle class White 'N' Black people is limited 'N' very rare

Ghetto people are required to navigate the White space as a condition of their existence

Whilst middle class White 'N' Black people avoid the ghetto they put up no resistance

'N' as the Black space is shaped by a history of marginalization 'N' limited social mobility

The White space, boasts cosmopolitan living, with colour blindness masquerading as civility

In the White space these 'code switchers' join clubs, attend churches that are wholly white

Whilst their children keep their blackness hidden, speaking 'ghetto talk' mainly at night

Meanwhile the 'Ghetto refugees' become established 'N' increasingly more assimilated

As the suburbs devour their Blackness, where they belong to 'White Space' incorporated

When Ghetto people enter the 'White space' they then become severely disrespected

As their White space cousins look on, do nothing 'N' watch their Blackness get rejected

As the colour line gets longer, Ghetto people begin to get agitated, angry 'N' confused

'N' they experience a 'field slave moment', which makes them feel battered 'N' very bruised

This 'field slave moment' attempts to put Ghetto people well 'N' truly in their place

In spite of knowing that the Black suburban 'code switchers' all come from the same race

Whether they live in the suburbs or the ghetto the skin tone they have in common is Black

'N' the police that stop them at night don't distinguish 'N' still put them under attack

In the White space, Black people are subject to social, cultural 'N' physical jeopardy

In the Black space ignorance of the 'code of the streets, will get no simple remedies

Meanwhile, the ghetto survives 'N' thrives though it appears to verge on self-destruction

'N' for White space visitors there's no 'street manual' or book with 'street instruction'

The ghetto is full of pain 'N' fear 'N' risks 'N' twists 'N' many diverse contradictions

There's bad man, gun man, angry yout's, honey traps, criminals 'N' ghetto restrictions

Civic authorities abdicate their responsibilities, as crime is tolerated 'N' media publicized

'N' as Ghetto people turn on each other, White space criminality is seldom if ever criticized

Respect for civil law erodes 'N' street justice emerges as part of 'the code of the street'

Where it's survival at all costs, making sure you maintain control over any loss or defeat

Meanwhile those who occupy the White space, look on with judgment 'N' pure disgust

Where biased assessments erode the ghetto's confidence, belief 'N' finally the trust

Black people in the White space then stigmatize the ghetto 'N' look the other way

The White space then puts the ghetto down 'N' code switchers have nothing left to say

The White space demands they dance, grin, smile, 'N' firmly know their subordinate place

As their 'deficit of credibility' may come out on top if they put on their minstrel face

Through performing 'N' grinning 'N' smiling these house Negros will do the masters dance

To show the ghetto stereotypes do not apply to them they're only given one small chance

Depending on how well they perform they have to wait to see if they pass the inspection

However, if they're too Black, too Ghetto, too smart, too clever the result is White rejection

When respected, a Black person who has a degree of moral sway benefits 'N' gains

Without it the 'deficit of credibility' is reinforced, applied, 'N unfortunately remains

When Black people lack the 'moral authority', those who offend them bear no shame

Meanwhile the code switcher loses credibility, then the White space forgets their name

In the White space, it matters little whether this level of acute disrespect is intended

You'll now be called 'an angry Black person' White space doesn't care if you're offended

The house slaves predicament unfolds gradually, is subtle, in many cases it's just minimal

Where moving to the White space puts them permanently on probation like a criminal

To occupy the White space, Black code switchers must invent 'N' create a different code

One where Blackness can be expressed, where there's no shame if you're from the road

People living in the White space must not stigmatize people from the ghetto who are Black

Or feel that when the Ghetto enters the White space, they will be under siege or attack

Unless the White space transcends the racialized barriers 'N' removes the moral barricades

The Ghetto will rise up, express their rage 'N' anger, becoming human hand grenades

Maybe it's time to rebuild the Ghetto 'N' show it's not a place to run from or to fear

Or White spaces must become contested, challenged, where they will finally disappear

Reflection

Generating work, having to be your own marketer, the endless round of funding deadlines, and so on, all eat into valuable creative time. Researchers are equally supposed to research, lecture, write, alongside being a businessperson, administrator, negotiator, pitcher of ideas. Making headway through the murky world of peer review is bad enough, but without a clear, focussed, and strategic approach in occupying the market place, a lot of researchers are destined to be rendered invisible, with piles of ideas languishing on shelves and occupying space within cupboards. For many researchers the issue of representation of their research, occupying the so-called market place, and generating 'reach and impact', is fraught with problems. If researchers are isolated from each other and seldom connect, with support networks fragmented, then the only options may be word of mouth and other uncoordinated pockets of creativity to generate work. If you are not part of those networks, in the know, or are living away from the nucleus of activity, it seriously restricts promoting important work. There needs to be a way for progressive researchers to distribute their work, which is run as a cooperative and which is self-determined in ethos. When one surveys the terrain of progressive researchers, there is no doubt that some great stuff is taking place. However, it is my view that energies can be better spent by not responding or reacting to the dictates of the peer review system or institutional 'cherry picking'. It is my view that performing reflexively can assist the researcher, research participants, and communities outside the academy in understanding the challenges faced by the researcher when conducting the research. This critical focus upon beliefs, values, professional identities, and how they affect, and are affected by, the surrounding cultural structures, is an overt social and political act. It should enhance the role of the researcher as a 'trusted other' by building confidence with the researcher's constituency. In essence, performance reflexivity becomes an integral, not a separate, element of the research inquiry itself.

Provocation

Quantitative or qualitative data stories to explain racial disparities within the criminal justice system? Whatever you choose, justify your choice.

Locating the Researcher: (Auto)-Ethnography, Race, and the Researcher

Chapter summary

This chapter calls for the embodied elements of the researcher's reflexive and auto ethnographic accounts to become both audible and visible through the expression of a 'performed story'. By immersing myself in the world of my own story and sharing it, I am making myself accountable to those I have engaged with along the way. Reflexivity and auto-ethnography, therefore, become acts of self-referral designed to generate some level of accountability between the researcher and the subjects of the inquiry.

Presentation of self

Mauthner and Doucet (2003) argue that though the importance of being reflexive is acknowledged within social science research, the difficulties, practicalities, and methods of doing it are rarely addressed. Thus, the implications of current theoretical and philosophical discussions about reflexivity, epistemology, and the construction of knowledge for empirical sociological research practice, specifically the analysis of qualitative data, remain underdeveloped. Mauthner and Doucet further argue that data analysis methods are not mere neutral techniques, but are imbued with theoretical, epistemological, and ontological assumptions – including conceptions of subjects and subjectivities, and understandings of how knowledge is constructed and produced. Similarly, Dean (2017) argues that reflexivity is vital in social research projects, but there remains relatively little advice on how to execute it in practice. Dean further calls for social science researchers to embrace the importance of thinking reflexively. Reflexivity is a vital source of my own continuing development given the complex nature of conducting race-specific research as a black male criminologist from an inner city background. Presenting 'self' in research, therefore, becomes an important modus operandi for researchers wanting to explore how a black art infused criminology can enhance or hinder notions of the academic identity. When an individual breaks the law, they are arrested, face a (performed) trial in front of an audience (jury), where characters (witnesses) are called into a staged scene (courtroom) to present both sides of the accused's life and behaviours (backstory). The resulting outcome is either freedom, or loss of liberty, if found guilty. Goffman's (1959) notion of the 'presentation of self' similarly acts as a 'researcher's metaphor' when presenting embodied experiences through performance. Goffman explored how theatrical performance may be applied to personal interactions and posited that individuals change or fix their appearance(s) and manner(s) when they come into contact with others in an attempt to control or guide the impression that others might make of them. I contend that by occupying racialized 'white spaces' I am called upon to perform notions of my blackness that, at times, become entangled in the site where my research is being conducted. In doing so, I have to construct insights and understandings where the intersectional mask I wear is removed and further interrogated (Turner, 1969). My embodied racialized persona, therefore, is presented through reflexivity, auto-ethnographic accounts, and performed in a space that reveals those interactions.

Reflexivity

The reflexive part of any research I undertake focuses on how my own racial identity impacts on my ability to remain objective. It also acts as an analytical tool from which to assess if my 'insider' position in the research would hinder my objectification throughout the research journey. Generally, insider researchers are those who chose to study a group to which they belong, while outsider researchers do not belong to the group under study. There are three key aspects of being an insider in the research domain:

- a significant understanding of a group's culture;
- the ability to interact naturally with the group and its members;
- a previously established and, therefore, greater relational intimacy with the group.

Taking on the role of the researcher often acts as a barrier that separates the insider from those in the setting you are researching. The insider positioning views the research process and products as 'co-constructions' between the researcher and the participants in the research; regard the research participants or respondents as 'active informants' to the research; and attempts to give 'voice' to the informants within the research domain. As such, these insider perspectives allow me to conduct research 'with' rather than 'on' the group, which contrasts starkly with outsider research perspectives. In embodying an insider role when undertaking my research created particular challenges that required careful consideration and appropriate responses. Total impartiality for me is impossible, but operating as the insider gives me a unique insight into the world of the subjects of the inquiry. Therefore, reflexive practice demands that the researcher relinquish a certain level of control within the research process, as a way of enabling the voices of the participants to be heard. As Duneier (2006) argues, participants in research should 'become authors of their own lives' and, by doing so, should experience some dignity within the research process. This is a view echoed by Becker, who states: 'We focus too much on questions whose answers show that the supposed deviant is morally in the right and the ordinary citizen morally in the wrong' (1967: 240). Therefore, the reflexive aspect of my research acts as a barometer, designed to identify the ongoing conflict between the objective and subjective aspects of the research itself. Frequently, the view has been expressed that occupying a space where the individual does not have to defend their cultural perspectives, linguistic codes, or expressions of blackness, becomes a liberating factor within the interview process. Gunarathum (2003) suggests that the race of the interviewer may have a level of subjectivity within the research process. I would argue that all research contains bias. However when researching one's own community, experience would suggest, that it is viewed with suspicion. Yet seldom do I see the same scrutiny placed upon white researchers conducting inquiries on white research participants.

Masking

Dunbar (1892) explores this notion of 'ontological reflection' where he writes:

> we wear the mask that grins and lies;
> it hides our cheeks and shades our eyes,
> this debt we pay to human guile;
> with torn and bleeding hearts we smile. (Dunbar, 1892: 167)

Dunbar's verse highlights a deep psychic challenge for researchers such as me, as the wearing of the racialized mask undermines positive constructs of myself, which in turn restricts me becoming 'the author of my own life' (McAdams, 1988). Dunbar's image of 'torn and bleeding hearts' further suggests that, in spite of the pain and burden of an oppressive history of slavery, colonialism, and racism, I am forced to put on a 'brave face', to don a mask, in order to survive black oppression and subsequent subordination in predominantly white spaces. The need for me to reveal my own truths, therefore, becomes significant if I am to transcend my 'racial subordination' within academia and the wider research community. DeFranz and Gonzalez (2014) argue that the embodiment of black performance socially emerges as a consideration about how we begin to name the mechanism(s) of black presence, alongside presenting a counter-narrative that can decentralize oppressive research paradigms. Denzin (2014) offers a supportive voice to the dilemma of critical researchers by seeing performance-based human disciplines as contributing to social change and cultural politics. As Chang (2008) reminds us, if auto-ethnography is about self-narrative it should transcend mere narration of 'self' to engage with cultural analysis and personal interpretation. This, in my view, not only legitimizes performing my research blackness as a political act, but it is a position that white academics must engage with as a way of accounting reflexively for their whiteness. I similarly argue that when staged performance becomes an element in the representation of research data, the physical performance is a powerful translation from the page to the stage. The validity of the words spoken or physicalized has the power to evoke emotional responses from the observer (audience). I believe that reflexivity constructed through performance is a powerful tool for gaining insight, understandings, and the perceived depiction of the lived realities of the researcher by 'breaking the fourth wall'.

Breaking the fourth wall

The representation of my 'self' using performance uses the theatrical tradition of 'breaking the fourth wall'. The term 'fourth wall' applies to the imaginary invisible wall at the front of the stage in a theatre through which the audience sees the action in the world of the play. The term signifies the suspension of disbelief by the audience, who are looking in on the action through the invisible wall. The audience thus pretends that the characters in the story are 'real living' beings in their own world, and not merely actors performing on a stage or studio set, or written words on the pages of a book. In order for the fourth wall to remain intact, the actors must also, in effect, pretend that the audience does not exist, by staying in character at all times and by not addressing the audience members directly. When I speak my data directly to an audience, I embody myself through the intersection of the physical, emotional, oral, political, and cultural. In doing so I reveal myself. In my junior days as a researcher, it was not uncommon for me to write reflexively from a standpoint of revealing my inner thoughts, biases, and other related experiences purely on paper. By extending my researcher vernacular using a creative process such as data verbalization to inform the presentation of (my) self, I locate those experiences within an open and vulnerable space, open to gaze and scrutiny. Performing reflexively, therefore, is about finding strategies to question not just my attitudes, thought processes, values, assumptions, prejudices, and habitual actions, but it moves (my)self beyond someone who merely undertakes reflection as practical exercise with little or no accountability.

Incorporation

Emirbayer and Desmond (2012) recognize that our understanding of the sociological order will remain unsatisfactory if we fail to turn our analytic gaze back upon ourselves and inquire critically into the hidden presuppositions that shape our thought. However, for reflexivity to be employed widely in the interest of pursuit of a series of truths, researchers must acknowledge reflexive thinking as much more than observing how our respective social positioning affects and impacts on the process of analysis. Mills (1959) sees the challenge before us is to develop a methodology that allows us to examine how the private troubles of individuals are connected to public issues and to public responses to those troubles. Similarly, Denzin and Giardina

(2017) express the view that qualitative researchers of all traditions are ideally equipped to reach beyond the wall of the academy, to engage competing publics, and to conduct research that changes the course of historical presence. Denzin (2010) further expresses the view that each generation must articulate its epistemological, methodological, and ethical stance toward critical inquiry. It is here I would like to turn my attention to indigenous ways of knowing. Within the scientific methods, the absence of a spiritual role within research further exacerbates the hegemonic assumptions that, at times, becomes the bedrock of Western forms of knowledge production. Brown and Strega (2005) assert that indigenous ways of knowing are inextricably linked to indigenous ways of doing by honouring the oral tradition of the ancestors expressed through storytelling. Ellingson (2017) presents a view that all research depends on the participant's participation, but that some participatory approaches share power and control with participants. Sharing power and control enables bodies to move freely, less constrained by the embodied power of researcher academic credentials and emphasizes the value of participants' perspectives and knowledge that is grounded in their daily lives. Therefore, indigenous researchers confront scientific researchers who ignore or render ancestral input into the research process null and void. How does the co-creation of meanings describe how a person comes to understand reality? Namely, what if those complex meanings of describing reality are rooted in ancient traditions? Alvesson and Skoldberg (2009) feel that serious attention paid to the different kinds of linguistic, social, political, and theoretical elements are woven together in the process of knowledge development, during which empirical material is constructed, interested, and written. Ultimately it is the researcher as storyteller who must take the ingredients of the research story, mould them, and share them in a unique and authentic way.

Eminent qualitative research advocate Norman Denzin argues that for 'subordinated voices' to be heard, they must be 'helped to speak'. Equally as important is the view of another important communications scholar, Arthur Bochner, who writes in his book *Coming to Narrative* about 'listening to different voices and trying to express your own, about trying to muster the courage to speak the unspoken even if it terrifies you' (2014: 315). Both Denzin and Bochner highlight the need for all of us to reveal our 'own truths' and to tell our own stories if we are to transcend the limitations imposed on us or, in turn, what we impose on ourselves. Denzin further argues for performative social science paradigms that provide some new answers to old problems. In responding to issues of power and inequality, Denzin calls for the construction of counter-narratives that will enable the subordinated individual or community to both narrate and interpret their lived reality through the dramatization of data.

Auto-ethnography

Qualitative interviewing involves a continuous process of reflection on the research. 'Reflexivity' is the process of examining both oneself as researcher and the research relationship. Reflexivity involves examining one's conceptual baggage, assumptions and preconceptions, and how these affect research decisions. Doing this enables personal thoughts, feelings, stories, and observations to give a greater understanding of the social context that is being studied. Denzin (2014: 6) considers that auto-ethnographic work 'must always be *interventionist*, seeking to give notice to those who may not be allowed to tell their story or who are denied a voice to speak'. Adams et al (2017) see auto-ethnography as a research method that uses personal experience ('auto') to describe and interpret ('graphy') cultural texts, experiences, beliefs, and practices ('ethno'). Auto-ethnographers believe that personal experience is infused with political/cultural norms and expectations, and they engage in rigorous self-reflection – typically referred to as 'reflexivity' – in order to identify and interrogate the intersections between the self and social life. Understanding auto-ethnography requires working at the intersection of *auto*biography and *ethnography*. Using this approach, therefore, is a 'critical response' to the alienating effects on both researchers and audiences of impersonal and abstract claims of truth generated by research practices that do not validate the 'subjective experiences' of the researcher. Important here is how performance 'auto ethnography' can give participants of the research inquiry a deeper insight into the researcher's experiences, processes, and methods, as a way of increasing the participatory nature of the research itself. In doing so, the researcher demonstrates their own positioning in an open and transparent manner. Spry (2001) argues for the emancipatory potential of auto-ethnographic performance as a method of inquiry. Park-Fuller (2000) likewise sees auto-ethnography as a form of critique regarding contested meanings of self and culture. Performing reflexively can assist the researcher, research participants, and communities outside of the academy in understanding the challenges faced by researchers. The importance of being reflexive within social science research – the difficulties, practicalities, and methods of doing it – are rarely addressed in relation to researching the racialization of crime. It is important when looking at the issues of researcher reflexivity that they are seen as not merely neutral techniques, but are imbued with subjective, theoretical, epistemological, and ontological assumptions of how knowledge is constructed and produced. In essence, performing reflexivity becomes an integral, not a separate, element of the research enquiry itself. Mauthner and Doucet (2003) argue that while the importance of being reflexive is acknowledged within social science research, the difficulties, practicalities, and methods of doing it are rarely addressed. Thus, the implications of current theoretical and philosophical discussions about reflexivity, epistemology, and the construction of knowledge for empirical sociological research practice, specifically the analysis of qualitative data, remain underdeveloped. Mauthner and Doucet further argue that data analysis methods are not mere neutral techniques, but are imbued with, theoretical, epistemological, and ontological assumptions – including conceptions of subjects and subjectivities, and understandings of how knowledge is constructed and produced.

Passages

For those of you who want to develop an auto-ethnographic approach to understanding your reflexive experiences, I am proposing a three-stage approach in the gathering of your personal data: *remembering*, *reframing*, and *re-evaluation*.

- *Remembering* is the use of memory as a way of recalling significant things, periods of your life, important people, etc. This process pieces together a past that has either been forgotten or blocked. Things will emerge and throw up many personal unresolved issues, which will also bring out a wide range of responses. In moving through the exercises, it is crucial to provide a balance between painful and uplifting memories.
- *Reframing* is the way we extend the way we use memory to develop new perceptions and differing points of view of ourselves. This section helps us look at deeply into who we are from the point of view of others. By doing this, we will hopefully be able to appreciate past mistakes, as well as acknowledging some of the good things we have contributed to the lives of others.
- *Re-evaluation* is projecting thoughts and ideas into the future. It gives a new purpose in life, so we can plan a new strategy. Having looked at our past, through our own experiences, and those of people we have affected, we can start to piece together a new route to spiritual liberation, and start to free ourselves of our internal oppression.

Re-evaluation is all about challenging ourselves, asking questions, and providing answers. By doing this, we are taking responsibility for shaping our own destiny and not leaving it to others.

Owning your story makes us human, reveals our imperfections, and connects us to others who have been through, or have experienced, things that are common to all of us. In owning our story we can demonstrate to the world that we are not alone in our silences.

Presenting your auto-ethnography

I am also aware that not everyone is confident in the ability to present their own auto-ethnography. This next section will hopefully assist you in looking at some of the key considerations when telling you story.

- *Have courage*: The journey towards owning your story takes courage. In spite of being an experienced storyteller, it is never easy when it comes to my own personal stories. Courage means stepping out of your comfort zone and giving yourself permission to share your experiences. By doing so, you have chosen to present yourself in ways that will lead to healing and transformation. As my sister would say 'be kind to yourself'. Do not rush. Come to your desire to tell your story in your own time.
- *Know your story*: Knowing your story is not just about memorizing the content. It is about understanding the world of your story, its characters, and the hidden meanings. Failure to do will result in your audience not getting the key messages or losing interest if your story goes off track.
- *What is the mood of the story*: As the driver of your story, it is your responsibility is to make it fresh, interesting, vibrant, and certainly not predictable. You should create the mood of your story much the same as an orchestra does with music. As the storyteller, you are in charge of shaping the direction of your story.
- *Act naturally*: Gestures adds interest and emphasis to the telling of your story. If you are nervous or awkward, start slowly. Add movements and gestures as you journey through your story.
- *Make eye contact*: A great way to help calm your nerves is to make eye contact with one person in the audience. Speak only to them. When you have looked at them long enough to feel you have made a connection, move on to another person, and then another.
- *Show your feelings*: You may normally be reserved, but as this is your story, open with a smile. Show your audience you are happy to

share your information with them. Facial expressions add power to your words.

- *Make yourself heard*: Make sure you speak loudly enough so that everyone can hear you. When presenters are nervous they often speak faster. Try to speak slowly and clearly, so your audience can understand every word. Finally, consider the pitch of your voice. Too much variation is distracting. Too little is monotonous. Aim for consistency with some variation when it is appropriate to the content.
- *Be energetic*: One thing I have learned is an enthusiastic storyteller will get a standing ovation, applause, and appreciation. An audience wants to get excited, enthused, challenged, and entertained all at the same time. If you understand the mood, temperament, and tempo of your story, you should be able to pace yourself and the energy required to have the maximum impact on your audience.
- *Become the characters*: If your story contains numerous characters it is critical for you to present their traits, mannerisms, gestures, and differences, as a way of enabling the audience to know who is who in the story.
- *Make it interesting*: Simple as this sounds, making a story interesting requires great skill. It requires you, the storyteller, to gauge the mood of the audience and to match the delivery to ensure there is a satisfactory outcome. To ensure you make your story interesting, lose yourself in the world of the story.
- *Respect your audience*: Do not lose your temper or insult the audience if it is not going your way. If you tell the story well and understand your audience, then there should be no problem.

There have been so many times when my academic identity has been bound up with my institution trying to erode 'my story', my sense of authenticity', and the history of those elements that inform it. Basking in the glory of passing my doctorate, I began the arduous task of reflecting on the events surrounding my transition from criminologist to academic. At that time there was no tenure or eager university department awaiting my services. Even more disconcerting is knowing that my role as a researcher and chronicler of the lives black men at times relegated me to the academic 'subs bench'. Imagine, Michael Jordan, because of his talent, being told he could never get on court? And when he does being told he is not allowed to handle the ball. There were, of course, fleeting moments where the occasional black scholar in the United Kingdom broke through for a period of time, but as the glass ceiling descends, like a vulture catching its prey, I was not one of them. At times when I did break through, there was a level of silent hostility where repeated insinuations became the basis of arguing that my connection to the streets would make me 'go native'. When I then responded by informing them that the streets were, and always would be, part of my own chosen proximity into researching the world of black men in prison and the community, the conversations tended to lead down a blind alley or I was ignored completely. In assessing the situation I have come to the conclusion that if I cannot get access to the club of elite criminologists, then maybe I should set up my own. As a trusted colleague once told me, "don't pick the food off someone else's menu. Instead write your own menu."

Reflection

My location to my participants was and is still not fixed in organized space. My encounters take place on street corners, shopping centres, churches, and numerous other communal spaces. Each day I am surrounded by extraordinary people who do not desire to be subjects of a research inquiry that is designed to shed light onto things that they themselves have had no consultation over. So I decided to canvas community opinion about my work as a criminologist in relation to operating within the confines of the inner city. There is no one version of individuals but many adaptions and formations of self. So, by becoming the author of your own life, you are choosing to write, direct, and star in your own narrative and, by doing so, experience some dignity within your research process. By the right to narrate I mean to suggest the creation of a space where you are free to represent yourself. This is a process that involves seeing yourself less as the outsider and more of experiencing life from a differing perspective, not defined according to the dictates of other privileged positions. Maybe it is more about joining with others, reaching out to those in the same situation as you, to form a union or, more importantly, to keep reminding yourself why you are doing what you are doing. As we conclude this small journey, I would like to suggest that the criminological project is both incomplete and lacking unless there is a wider validation and inclusion of the contribution of excluded and marginalized non-white and progressive white scholars when looking at the racialization of crime, as well as crime as a whole. A need for a criminological counter-narrative is now required. It is to this end that I am calling for a 'black arts infused criminology'.

Provocation

What are your thoughts regarding using a critical race reflexive methodology when exploring your biases pertaining to racialization of crime and criminal justice?

Towards a Black Arts Infused Criminology

Chapter summary

Presenting a counter-narrative to the dominant majoritarian narrative that currently exists will not only challenge the myth of criminological meritocracy, but expose criminological white privilege in the process. By placing 'race and the racialization of crime' at the centre of their analysis and moving away from paradigms that hold whiteness within criminology as the norm, critical race criminologists must identify research agendas that incorporate collective actions taken by an inclusive cohort of activists scholars committed to the struggle for academic validation, transformation, and change.

Racialized perceptions

Gabbidon et al (2004) understand that in spite of the moderate gains made to increase the inclusivity of black scholars in relation to criminology and criminal justice, more needs to be done to incorporate perspectives and theoretical ideas that deviate from so-called 'mainstream criminology'. Fanon (1952: 3) begins to unpack and set a tone for further discussion when he writes:

> The white man is sealed in his whiteness
> The Black man in his blackness
> We shall seek to ascertain the directions of this 'dual narcissism
> And the motivations that inspire it.

The significance of Fanon's position is in the envisioning of a critical race criminological imagination that requires a struggle to end any criminological hegemony that desires to subordinate the black voice within the discipline. Zinn (1959) has a word of caution for so-called mainstream criminology's currently monopoly on the discipline and argues that the day-to-day discipline centring on issues of race and racialization should depend on the compliance of a vast number of people. When that compliance is withdrawn, en masse, even force is inadequate to hold back the impulse for justice. Zinn clearly understands that exclusion of a diverse range of criminological theories and perspectives can only lead to division and internal conflict among those who ultimately have one common aim, to ensure the understandings and insights around crime and criminal justice are strong, unified, and robust. Gilroy (1987) argues that 'race' must be retained as an analytic category, not because it corresponds to any biological or epistemological absolute, but because it refers investigation to the power that collective identities acquire by means of their roots in tradition. Barak (1991) suggests that implicit bias within criminal justice and criminology suppresses the socio-historical context for making sense of the 'black experience' in relation to crime and justice as a whole. In turn, Barak expresses the view that this suppression not only distorts the overall perspectives in criminal justice, but interferes with the emergence and development of a wider global conversation on crime and justice as a whole. I argue that these omissions further isolate marginalized groups that, in turn, reinforces racial stratification and polarization. In essence, it reinforces society's classed, raced, and gendered constructs. Covington (1995) sees the racialization of academic criminology as a conduit that can be used to justify increased control of individual black criminals in the larger society. These controls can be extended to encompass similar persons who are not involved in crime. Criminalization of race is important because it means that, since racial identities are constructed, they can be reconstructed to include decriminalized identities. Racialization in the criminal justice context has two conceptual problems.

- There is an over concentration on opinion leaders and policy makers. They are given too much say on the construction of racial identities. They not only construct whiteness but blackness.
- Racialized groups have a limited number of ways to respond to a history of oppression and structural constraints. Racialized populations are not thought of as making choices, because no choices are available to them or because they lack the consciousness to do so.

Failure to create a more equitable narrative within the discipline of so-called 'mainstream' criminology will merely promote and reinforce a subordinate status for excluded and marginalized criminological voices, which will continue to render a wider debate invisible. This bringing together of the symbiosis of black art and black criminology, may generate a black arts infused criminology that will provide a platform to bring to the fore the black contribution to criminology that is currently rendered invisible. The need to transcend the confines of the 'ivory tower' demands qualitative researchers to heed this call to arms for those of us who believe in the polyphonic relationship between critical inquiry, social justice, and the racialization of crime. In spite of an array of new books attempting to contextualize 'race and the racialization crime' within the discipline of criminology, seldom do they direct their attention to a wider and more inclusive global criminology that gives voice to excluded, marginalized, and indigenous criminological perspectives, which is both limiting and troubling in equal measure. With issues such as racial disproportionality and mass incarceration, racial profiling, police–black community relations, the rise of the far right, alongside the media acting as a racializing agent in areas of criminological investigation such as 'urban inequality' and 'gangs', becoming prominent across the world, there is a further questioning of how these inward-looking perspectives renders others subordinate. Equally as significant is exploring ways to create space for a new wave of unified global critical voices to emerge. It is, therefore, incumbent on this chapter to look at this omission as a way of recontextualizing the understanding of race and the racialization of crime within so-called mainstream criminology as a whole. Olusoga (2016: xx) adds to this conundrum where he writes: 'Many [of the] most significant black figures are mute, silenced by a lack of written sources.' Olusoga further reveals how white historians have failed to locate the historical representation of crime and punishment within a wider racialized or global context. Further questions emerge: Why is it that so-called mainstream criminology has largely failed to include or examine a more inclusive global-historical context within the overall analysis of crime as a whole? And, furthermore, What are the implications for understanding wider global contexts/perspectives within the discipline of criminology itself? For the scholar or student, whose interests lie within the study of those wider global contexts/ perspectives within criminology there are available few comprehensive courses or significant modular content based on a binary of exclusive– inclusive, rendering a more culturally competent discipline invisible.

Towards a black arts infused criminological imagination

By moving towards a black arts infused criminology it is intended that progressive criminologists will actively ensure that their contribution to the so-called mainstream discipline of criminology is not rendered invisible, null and void, as well as transcending the Global North–South. However, the invisibility experienced by many non-white scholars like myself is yet another stark reminder of the discipline's unapologetic colour-blind rendering within a discipline that seems to have little or no accountability regarding the importance of social and racial justice goals set within a global context. It is, therefore, proposed that this new movement operates beyond the confines of mainstream criminology much the same as the black arts movements cited in this book did. It is further proposed to locate and contextualize those ideas in relation to the understanding of crime as a whole. Gilroy (2008) argues that the racialization of crime requires a detailed historical investigation that will raise further and more speculative questions. Gilroy goes further and expresses the view that historically 'the left' has failed to appreciate the complexities of black life and discounts the impact of structural racism within its overall class analysis.

Transcending bias

The need, therefore, to reinvigorate discussions around the necessity for a racialized counter-narrative within criminology becomes important here. It could be argued that so-called mainstream criminology reproduces a biased account of crime and criminal justice, which in itself does little to ameliorate racial disadvantage within the discipline itself, alongside playing a marginal role in contesting racial disadvantage within criminal justice systems across the world. Mauer (1999) expresses the view that the responsibility for alleviating racial disparities in criminal justice needs to be addressed appropriately through both policy and practice at all levels of government, informed by effective criminological inquiry that is inclusive of a diverse range of perspectives. The Home Office (2006) also reveals an acknowledged level of racial disparities within the UK criminal justice system, which requires a national conversation into what shapes our beliefs, insights, understandings, and perceptions around the racialization of crime in relation to the study of crime as a whole. In spite of the sheer volume of research, journal articles, and other related academic literature emerging from the US, the context, orientation, and understanding of a broader 'race and racialization of crime' project within a global context is sadly lacking. For the scholar or student, whose criminological interests lie within the study of the realms of race and racialization of crime, there are limited options in terms in terms of courses, modular content, or even relevant texts. How then does the study of race and racialization of crime impact on the ways in which we view criminality emerging from global communities? And how does this impact influence how we view crime as a whole in a global context?

Don't hide history

The need to theorize using racialized paradigms that challenge implicit bias within the discipline of criminology should become a rallying cry for all criminologists who have grown tired of criminological theorizing that ignores racialized discourses. Agozino (2010) points out that criminology as a discipline must learn from Africa's history in order to advance the discipline itself. Agozino argues forcibly that an 'African centred criminology' should focus less on the unravelling of the individual's motivation towards crime, but instead address the wider structural determinants that generates the condition from which criminality emerges. Agozino's position must be seen as a rallying cry for those criminologists who feel that the histories of slavery and colonialism cannot be disconnected or divorced from African people's overall engagement with, and connection to, their criminality. Important here is in the recognition that years and years of systematic abuse of non-white and indigenous people could account for the kind of criminal adaptions that leads to criminality. Chilisa (2012) sees that the concerns and worldviews of the oppressed and colonized should be understood by them through their own assumptions, concerns, and perspectives. Chilisa further sees that researchers and related disciplines that aim to silence, marginalize, and alienate transformative perspectives must be part of a process of decolonization coming from scholars within disciplines who see an important part of their role to contest and challenge oppressive and restrictive paradigms that seek to reinforce racialized privileges. In seeking redress, Chilisa concludes, there may be a level of restitution that enables minority concerns to be differently situated. Repositioning the epistemological concerns around criminology to be more inclusive of minority perspectives means recognizing that rigorous academic research is impotent without applied efforts and social policy that empowers marginalized and other disenfranchised people worldwide. It is about engaging with the experiences of the historically oppressed, alongside acknowledging the often troubling complexities inherent in undertaking such a mission.

Metaphors

In this context, prophetic research is a metaphor for research that studies the nuances of race and racialization within criminology, as well as expanding the discussion on crime as a whole beyond our current views and understandings. The need to understand to what extent race and the racialization of crime impact on all stratas of criminal justice systems becomes important here. To address this issue directly, I am suggesting that there is a need to produce a counter-narrative to bring to account implicit biases within so-called mainstream criminology. There is also a need to speak out against those conservative criminologists who seek to stifle a wider debate within the academy concerning the need for a more diverse lens when looking at race and the racialization of crime, much the same as feminist criminology has done in relation to the advancement of women within the study of criminology. Bell (1992) further advocates for racial reform within the criminal justice system that examines how differential racialization is produced, maintained and sustained. This in my view has implications for criminology as a discipline and the claims it makes regarding race and the racialization of crime.

The Global North–South divide

Cuneen and Rowe (2016) argue that there have been limited attempts to consider the theoretical and practical implications of indigenous understandings and approaches to the discipline of criminology. They further argue that criminology is equally as slow in recognizing the importance of understanding the way in which colonial effects are perpetuated through knowledge control, particularly in relation to criminal justice systems. Carrington et al (2016) similarly argue that criminologists of the Global South have by and large accepted their subordinate role within the global organization of knowledge to the detriment of occupying a prominent role within the wider global discipline of criminology itself. The assertions of both Carington et al and Cuneen and Rowe provide an important entry point for positioning intersectionality as a key theoretical framework when considering a black arts infused criminology. Crenshaw (1999) argues that intersectionality is the understanding that human beings are shaped by the interaction of different social locations, within a context of connected systems and structures of power. Crenshaw further argues that through such interactions independent forms of privilege and oppression are created. It is my view that any future progression of the discipline of criminology must not only account for its implicit biases, but must also strive towards wider social and racial justice goals. Indeed my observations, connection to, and engagement with, the criminal justice system over the last three decades would suggest that the current so-called mainstream framing of race and the racialization in relation to looking at crime as a whole is deeply flawed, inward looking, and does little to respond to the shifting patterns of racial inequality within a global context. It is also my assertion that, unless we comprehend how notions of the 'other' are constructed and acted upon, the discipline of so-called mainstream criminology will merely continue to re(produce) and (re)inforce a continuing legacy of racialized dominance. Equally as important is to reconcile the contextual criminological understandings and differences that underpin the binary of the Global North–South divide. Therefore, this criminological hegemony requires the development of a criminological counter-narrative as a way of revising the discipline as a whole. It is further evident that the lack of unification, awareness, or connections between Global North–South criminological theorists, writers, academics, etc is something that must be bridged if we are to have a truly inclusive and more rounded representation of criminology in the future. In essence, it is envisioned that by bridging the Global North–South divide, we will be able to engage in a dialogue based less on separation, privilege, and cultural dominance, but one of mutual respect for other perspectives that are not being seen, heard, or acknowledged within the current Global North dominance within contemporary mainstream criminology. Here I would like to reveal the positive impact that engagement with creative rehabilitative processes can have on one black offender. Although a singular art activity in itself may not be enough to arrest offending behaviour, creating space to process the experience of incarceration, combined with appropriate support and guidance, can lead to a positive outcome for a high risk offender's re-entering the community.

Case example: JB's journey

I was approached by JB after his release from prison, as he wanted to share his story with someone he could trust. JB was a 32-year-old reformed ex-gang member from Birmingham (West Midlands). He had served six and a half years in prison for gang-related offences.. JB was informed of the nature of the interview, where I advised him that he could withdraw any stage. Eight key elements were identified in my process as an interviewer. These elements were predicated on the notion that, as I was operating in an insider position, my own sense of identification as a black man would be important here. Those eight elements were as follows.

- *Connectivity*. My understanding of black/street vernacular enabled me to gain access to JB's cultural and linguistic codes.
- *Perception*. My 'rite of passage' was rooted in the perception that JB had of my politics, knowledge of black history, culture, and blackness. I thereby gained a level of credibility that encouraged and increased his motivation to be interviewed.
- *Mediation*. Based on my ability to gain credibility, the exchange of ideas was less of a scientific process and one where JB told me his story in a relaxed and non-threatening way.
- *Negotiation*. Throughout the interview there was a sense of ongoing negotiation. Once again, the credibility I had gained made negotiation that much easier. There were revelations that at times were private, painful, and awkward. Accommodating JB was central to the process and exchange between interviewer and interviewee.
- *Exchange*. At times, JB wanted to ask me questions. This tended to take place either before the interview started or directly after.
- *Discharge*. At times, JB's views came out in a range of emotive ways. When telling his stories, some powerful things were expressed that occasionally resulted in a few tears, angry outbursts, or long silences.
- *Revelation*. When telling his truths, JB became very vulnerable. Keeping myself together was also an important part of reassuring him that it was a safe space to let out the deep feelings and strong emotions that came to the surface.
- *Closure*. In the debriefing that followed each interview, it was important to bring closure to the interview. Both JB and I sat in silent contemplation for a few moments.

Sharing the process is to highlight that what was taking place was not only intergenerational but also became generative, as my interaction with JB enabled me to pass on some valuable insights from my own experiences that would have remained hidden if I was interviewing him in prison.

The interview

When JB could not find positive opportunities and when other resources were not available to him, crime became an option.

The pressure of expectation placed on JB from family, friends, and community made things worse when his access to the 'social structures' blocked possible meaningful and productive opportunities. With severely limited education and skills, JB had little opportunity to participate in the civic life of the community and became a product of the streets and indifferent to the law.

JB: I was crap at school. Always fighting and angry all the time at the teachers. It's only when I left school I found out I was dyslexic. Everyone thought I was stupid. Dad wasn't around. Nuff and sisters. Plus mum did more than one job. So I never got any attention. No guidance. All my friends at the time were going through the same thing. So it was just a matter of time before I started to stray. I used to sneak out of the house. Back then my brothers and sisters used to tell my mum, which made it worse. Basically I was out of control. That's when the streets called me out.

JB connected to the streets and used criminality to challenge existing social structures that still excluded him. By doing so, JB created an alternative social structure, namely that of joining a gang. To be part of a gang JB had to be prepared to lose his life in exchange for the gains he received from criminality. To gain access to the gang, JB met with a senior gang member and was issued with challenges. The 'code of the streets' is where JB found respect, exhibited toughness, was fearless, and operated with loyalty, which were the benchmarks for measuring the resources he had to possess in order to be part of his gang. JB saw this code of the streets, or 'on road', as part to a dangerous game, where he exercised control over territory with others.

JB: I was about 13 when I started doing robberies and burglary. Never got caught. It wasn't anything major, but after a while certain bigger manz in the community heard about what was doing. I suppose I got a bit of a rep. I wasn't interested in gangs at that point in my life, just making money, coz mum never had any. At school things got bad and I got expelled for fighting. That's when I decided to join a gang. Never went back to school and got deep into the gang runnings. Had to do some dark stuff to get in, but once I did, they became my new family. I became like a mad man. I didn't care about anything.

In spite of numerous attempts by his family to stop his being involved in the gang, JB had a stronger allegiance to his new and extended gang family. Eventually, his involvement in criminal activity landed him in trouble; he was caught, convicted, and sent to prison. The development of JB's identity while in prison was part of an ongoing socialization process shaped by experiences with his family, community, school, and group and social affiliations. While change in the prison environment required JB's new prisoner identity to change, he initially found it disturbing and difficult. For JB, the desire to change for the better while in prison was undermined by having to fashion a new identity based on the 'prison code'.

JB: When I heard the judge give me nine-year sentence, I was gutted. I saw my family in court, crying. I felt ashamed. Trust me. When they took me down, I knew my nightmare had just begun. But at the time I still thought I was a bad man.

JB disliked the prison environment intensely and did not want to repeat old patterns of behaviour. However, he had not acquired the tools required to go back as a productive member of his community. As the primary purpose of prison is punishment, the confinement, containment, and security, created the kind of social order that at times pushed JB into adapting the prison code; using menace, fear, violence, and the fear of violence governed much of his behaviour:

JB: To tell the truth I didn't feel anything in prison. On road you can't show weakness, so you have to block stuff out, or you can't be a soldier. I was cool for a while. Rollin' with the older guys in prison, doin' all sort of crazy shit. I was makin' money, had nuff women and I had the lifestyle. I thought I had it locked. Got away with it. Then some proper madness went down, and then it really hit. I was in prison.

After being punished even further and falling out with other men in the prison, JB viewed his intended new journey and the road ahead as tricky. He also felt that if he conquered the difficulties he faced he would become a hero in the eyes of his family, friends, and, in turn, the community. However, when faced with the challenges and difficulties of prison life, JB's incentive to 'go straight' was thwarted and met with opposition, and he further felt ill-equipped to meet the new challenges that lay ahead. JB now came to the attention of the prison's most feared individual, who ran his wing with menace, and who commanded brutal loyalty with intimidating respect, much the same as the gang leader on the streets. The resulting outcome nearly pushed him back into becoming desensitized as a survival mechanism. JB now became quite withdrawn and fearful of life in prison. This became a turning point for his transformation:

JB: I hated prison. Reminded me of school. Only this time I white screws instead of teachers. Plus you had to deal with manz from other endz, as well as beefin' with racist prisoners. It was a mad one. Couldn't take the loneliness or isolation. Hardly got any visits and when I did, it was pure arguments with my mum. None of my old crew ever came to see me. Neither did my nan as she was too upset to see me. There were times when I thought I was goin' crazy.

JB spent a lot of time reflecting and delving into his troubled past, as he knew failure to confront his inner demons would result in perpetuating the same type of behaviour that landed him in prison in the first place. It was at this point that JB underwent a crisis that acted as a turning point for his soon-to-be new journey. He discovered the prison library, the art room, and supportive prison staff:

JB: It then I started to read. It was even harder trying to read when I got older, but I had nuff time on my hands. So I went down the prison library and took it slow at first. I was pissed at first, as they had no black books. In fact the only thing that was black whilst I was in jail, were the prisoners. However, the librarian saw something in me and encouraged me to continue with my reading.

Armed with a new consciousness and awareness, JB then turned to older prisoners for advice and guidance. In some respects they became like prison mentors, where wisdom, advice, and guidance were given to him as a way supporting him in his desire not to make their mistakes. JB now submerged himself in learning and art education, operated as a wing representative, and became a prison listener. Around the prison, both prisoners and prison officers noticed a shift in his behaviour. JB was now less anti-social, but developing more of a pro-social identity, which resulted in him undergoing a 'faith based conversion':

JB: After a couple of years I started doing some courses, engaged in art classes, and started to get my education sorted. I became a listener, wing rep, and I began to feel useful. I started writing to my mum, and she started to visit more. I felt different.

In spite of JB doing what was asked of him, his past reputation was ever present. His new-found status brought out adverse responses from some of his old friends, as well as other new prisoners who knew JB when he operated on the streets. The desire to go straight and keep his head down was constantly being challenged by JB having to renavigate the prison code with his change of status. Provocations, threats, and further intimidation, pushed JB to his limits:

JB: I suppose in a strange way prison made me think about my life. In some respects it was a good thing, coz I felt I was better than I used to be. However, I still used to get beef from my old bredrin's. They would call me names, try to physically intimidate me, and tried to make life hard for me. They struggled with accepting the changes I'd made. It didn't bother me at first, but after a while it started to get to me as it made me angry. I wouldn't understand why they would want to act this way knowing I was trying to be more positive with my life.

In some respects, JB was merely being tested by individuals, whose loyalty and support swung like a pendulum, resulting in periods of confusion and psychic conflicts, such as anxiety and depression. As the conflict between his loyalty to old friends and the desire to keep his head down grew, JB found himself in the segregation unit where he felt better able to avoid the distractions he was facing. However, the isolation, disconnection, and having too much thinking time on his hands, was a significant challenge for JB:

JB: When I look back on it, although I hated being on my own, I felt better. I read the bible, did my writing, and kept my mind active. Although I felt lonely, but I knew that it was because I was trying to break old habits. Also, there were some genuine people that I missed, but the thought of my freedom was bigger than my connection to people inside. After all we were all prisoners.

After a few tense weeks, psychological battles, and a deep longing to be free, JB eventually got his freedom, and was released from prison with time off for being a model prisoner. Things were on the up for JB. Internally, JB asked himself a range of new questions: Can I do this? Will I stay out of trouble? What if temptation comes back to me? Do I have the discipline to get me back on track? Will I get a job? Can I take care of my family? At this moment in the journey, the enormity of the task began to set in. JB left prison, was picked up by his mum, and driven through his old community, which had remained unchanged since he had been locked up. Emotionally, JB's thoughts fuelled his self-doubt – the euphoric moment of release contrasted as the fear of release and re-entry kicked in:

JB: So I came out. My mum picked me up. I remember I just hugged her. My little sister was there too. I felt good. Trust me. I'll be honest when I knew I was getting released I felt nervous as hell. It had been a long time. I know I had changed, but whilst I was inside was all the crap on road. I didn't know what I would be like.

JB knew that there would be a range of personal and professional support designed to boost his confidence, develop new skills, as well as urging him to be compliant with society's rules. Another close friend reassured JB that the destination towards desistance should be seen as a new adventure. This mentor equipped JB with some creative tools required to go straight and urged him to be courageous in the pursuit of acquiring a new status beyond the label 'ex-prisoner'. JB felt empowered and inspired to continue, but self-doubt still lurked within from the traumatic experiences of prison life. Although JB was free of the world he had left behind (prison), he had now returned to a new world (community), a place of wonder and marvel. Things had changed. The sweet smell and taste of freedom enabled JB to envision a new reality, where he could live in this special world, not only free, but knowing that the journey towards a new status would bring new rewards – employment, increased social bonds, and a restoration of positive masculine status. JB now encountered new challenges – a probation officer, an employment specialist, and old friends/rivals who taunted him. JB struggled with gaining employment, furthering his studies, managing family life, adjusting to life outside of prison, meeting old adversaries, and experienced the cumulative impact of everything around him.

JB: Although I'd got qualifications, had a good group of people around me, and I also had good links at my local Church. But I still felt weird. I never felt that nervous when I was

on road. I knew I couldn't go back to what I was. I kind of
felt with my faith I had nothing to worry about. I knew all
I wanted to do is come back into the community and do the
right thing. I didn't want no drama in my life. I felt ready.

JB knew that his ability or inability to negotiate these new challenges
would determine whether he continued the journey towards desistance
or recycled old patterns of behaviour that inevitably would land him
back inside. Several questions emerged for JB: Am I man if I back
down? If I can't make ends meet, does that lessen me? If I do go
straight, will the system really make me better off?

JB: I was completely alone with my thoughts. Internally, there
was a massive amount of confusion where I needed clarity.
However, the responsibility for making the necessary
changes was with me. It was at this moment that the skills
I developed in prison education via enhanced thinking
skills provision helped me out.

JB weighed up the pros and cons of his life, and assessed his options,
balanced against what tools he had to sustain and maintain his journey
towards his desistance. JB reflected on his family, real friends, children,
and, in turn, what freedom really meant to him. However, there were
new challenges that lay ahead. JB's old street adversaries provided the
tension of anxiety and fear post release.

JB: That feeling didn't last long. Things still looked the same.
I saw some my old bredrins' standin' on the same corner
I stood on all those years back. I felt bad. I couldn't believe it.

JB also reflected on his skills, abilities, hopes, dreams, and aspirations, and
connected that to a purpose that was culturally and spiritually driven. In
essence he discovered his 'generative self'. By doing so, JB discovered
that putting others' needs before his own brought a different reward.

JB: When I got to my mum's house, there were a few people
waitin for me, especially my nan. I cried. I didn't feel no
way. I was so relieved. I'll never forget my first night of
freedom. I couldn't sleep. I kept thinkin' about my bredrin's
in prison and what my future was gonna be. It took me
ages to get work and settle back into things. But my faith
kept me goin'.

JB decided that it was better to be poor and free, than be a slave to negativity. However, the fear of having to deal with the negative vested interests generated another layer of fear and self-doubt. The reward, although achievable, seemed a long way off. He decided to confront his old past and cut it off. In doing so, he encountered hostility, aggression, rejection, and conflict. JB engaged with a range of new people, who gave him access to a new life – faith leaders, sports and cultural practitioners, educators, employers, voluntary agencies. JB's 'social capital' was on the rise. In essence JB's heroism kicked in, as he realized that to fully desist he would have to make sacrifices. In essence, he started to place the needs of others above his own selfish individualism, which is generative in orientation:

JB: I'm gonna be honest probation didn't really help, plus my old bredrins were trying to rope me back in to the old ways, but I resisted the temptation, when it got rough. Some of the brothers had a barber shop, and I started doin' some trimmin' and made a little change to keep me goin'. Eventually me and some of the other brothers who'd become Christian opened a little shop, where we cut hair, sold books, and tried to do something in the community. That's how I met my wife, Beverly. I've now got a daughter, Naomi, my own place, and I'm goin' back to college to study business. I know there's a possibility that I can always get into trouble, but with the right support it's possible.

JB's new position had a new reward for him, namely community acceptance and a reincorporated status that validated his sense of masculine courage. JB had fashioned a new identity formed by the past, but shaped by journeying towards a new future. The label 'ex-prisoner' had now been both rejected and replaced with the reclamation of his own name, Jonathan. JB, now Jonathan, was reborn and celebrated making those choices that had made it possible. He now looked back on the journey and vowed never to return to the dark forest where he once resided. Jonathan became a mentor, and is still seen by a range of vested interests as now having value. The journey made had taken Jonathan from a position of a 'social liability' and turned him into a 'community asset'. Agnew (2006) argues that when criminals are asked why they offend, they typically do not place much emphasis on background factors. JB's story tried to account for his engagement in crime more holistically by recognizing why he engaged with criminal activity, as well as using his story to develop his own counter-narrative, which charted a new course in his life. JB's recounting of this series of 'episodes' was part of his epic journey as a 'hero' who willingly, and unwillingly, ventured beyond this known boundaries, met and defeated difficult challenges, then returned with a hard-won, precious gift, namely his freedom.

New identity

By reclaiming a new identity and improving his self-concept as a consequence of undertaking a mythic journey, he transcended his social liminality. McAdams (1988) maintains that individuals who can make sense of their lives in the form of a 'life story' or 'self-narrative' may be better able to transcend their 'at-risk status' and be reintegrated back into the community and ultimately desist. Therefore, journeying through the various stages of his life via narrative construction provided a perfect conduit for JB to cease all involvement with criminal behaviour. As discussed previously, Maruna and Roy (2006) suggest that life changes, such as desistance from crime, may be shaped by a process of 'knifing off' – the means by which individuals are thought to change their lives by severing themselves from detrimental environments. The challenge of returning ex-prisoners is much more than their physical relocation into their home communities. The real challenge of reintegrating former prisoners like JB back into the community is more psychological. Paternoster and Bushbay (2009) likewise argue that before an individual is willing to give up their working identity as a law-breaker, they must begin to perceive this identity as unsatisfying, thus weakening their commitment to it. They further argue that those wishing to quit crime are more likely to be successful at desistance if they are embedded in social networks that not only support their new identities and tastes but also isolate them from those who would oppose them quitting crime or induce them to continue in their criminal ways. By providing encouragement, opportunities, and structures through which they can function as full members of the community, returning prisoners like JB can become positive contributors to community life. These reintegration aspirations are built on two premises: first, that the returning prisoner has skills, abilities, and talents that can and should be used for the benefit of the community to which they return; and, consequently, second, that rather than seeing them as community liabilities, communities should view them, and enlist and deploy them, as community assets. Successful re-entry is about providing what has been missing in the lives of most returning prisoners and other marginalized individuals – a strong sense of connection. To promote a successful, positive return for former prisoners to their home communities, we must engage with their stories, which will increase their appreciation for the challenges facing the communities they have affected and then connect them to real and meaningful opportunities to make a difference and affect positive change. Important here is the consideration of the influence of local cultures and how membership of powerful street cultures fractures the possibility of young people like JB going straight. However, visual arts can repair the damage done by historical trauma to those who, unlike JB, have little or no support, post-release. The ability to contest this position of 'differential racialization' involves interrogating how the narrative of so-called mainstream contemporary criminology is produced, produces, or does not produce change. An existential question now arises: Who is best qualified to drive this counter-narrative forward? It may require those scholars who believe in the value of diversification in criminology to seek new, improved, and contemporary solutions in the way crimes are constructed, researched, analysed, and acted upon.

A black arts infused criminological imagination manifesto

How then does the discipline of so-called mainstream criminology engage in a critical dialogue that will ensure that theoretical criminological perspectives from global criminology scholars moves the discourse beyond mere 'identity politics'? A black arts infused criminology may provide a way forward, and comprises the following principles.

- A black arts infused criminological imagination is a shared pedagogical space from which to contest, challenge, and expose criminological theorizing that reinforces dominant ideological positions when looking at race and the racialization of crime and criminal justice systems that exclude, ignore, and render some criminological positions subordinate when looking at crime as a whole.
- A black arts infused criminological imagination will enable subordinated criminological perspectives to narrate, to interpret events in opposition to the dominant criminological narratives, while at the same time recognizing the complexity of race, racialization, colour blindness, white privilege, and implicit bias of crime/criminal justice systems within the discipline of criminology.
- A black arts infused criminological imagination will operate from critical race theory's two distinct storytelling paradigms – 'majoritarian

stories' told by privileged criminologists, and 'counter-stories' told by subordinated criminologists. Critical race theory intends to respond to this majoritarian story by critically evaluating how it reproduces its claims in relation to race, racialization, colour blindness, white privilege, and implicit bias of crime/criminal justice systems and criminology.

- A black arts infused criminology further envisions a bridging of the Global North–South divide within the discipline of so-called mainstream criminology itself. The Global North–South divide is a socio-economic and political divide. The Global North includes the US, Canada, Western Europe, developed parts of Asia, Australia and New Zealand, who share similar economic and cultural characteristics. The Global South, on the other hand, is made up of Africa, Latin America, and developing Asia, including the Middle East.

The reasoning behind these assertions is rooted in the understanding that there is a privileging of criminological perspectives and debates on race and the racialization of crime and criminal justice systems, while others are excluded, seldom heard, seen, or referred to, within so-called mainstream criminology. A possible explanation of to this invisibility could be that it as a consequence of implicit biases within the discipline itself, which further reproduces and reinforces privilege of some perspectives, while at the same time subordinating others. As a black scholar, the need to engage with my own sense of racial and cultural knowledge, the community I come from, and the subject of the inquiries, without the imposition of oppressive whiteness, becomes critical as I close this thought piece. Seldom, in my experience, is there a questioning of how white men research other white men, but I undergo a continual battle in having to justify my desire to research those who look like me. I have now listened to the spirit memories of my past warning me not to abandon my creative self. I searched my archives and (re)discovered a reworking of one of my all-time favourite pieces, *The Revolution Shall Not Be Televised* by the late, great Gil Scott Heron. This unification heralded a shift in both my consciousness and personal growth.

Digital Revolution

(Dedicated to Gil Scott-Heron)
You will not be able to stay in the comfort of
Your high-rise block or detached house in

The suburbs ... brothas and sistas ...
You will not be able to walk away ... run off ... or hide
You will not be able to smoke a spliff ... take crack ...
Place a bet or get drunk ...
The revolution shall not be brought to you
By Dixon's ... PC World ... Curry's ... The World
Wide Web or Email ...
The revolution will not show you
Satellite images of Black on Black crime ...
false consciousness ... Depression ... or a community
in crisis
The revolution shall not be brought to you
By Eddie Murphy ... Chris Rock or any other Black
comedian
Who believes that comedy kills pain
The revolution will not hide your ugly attitude
The revolution will not hide your fears
The revolution will not make your weave look better
The revolution will not make your sex drive improve
The revolution will not make you a better Christian
The revolution will not make you more acceptable to
White people
There will be no still images of single
Parent mothers 'N' Brothas passin' on
The virus to Sista's
There will be no software for the countless
victims of physical and sexual abuse who remain silent.
There will be no CD of the brotha who
Commits suicide in his cell as he struggles
To deal with a life sentence.
No amount of memory on the hard drive
Will be able to stop the yout' who explodes coz he's
had enough
The BBC will not be able to make a docu-soap about
ghetto life
And Executive Producers will be unavailable for comment
As they would have fled the scene ...
Makin' Uncle Toms
Scramble for the crumbs left behind
There will be no pictures of the police feedin'
An evenin' meal of baton ... boot ... and fist ...
To a brotha who was in the wrong place at the

Wrong time with the wrong colour skin
There will be no repeat performances after the watershed
There will be no pictures of upwardly mobiles
Having their superiority complexes destroyed
by a young brotha who wants what they have as he's
Tired of being fed lies and false promises.
There will no photographs using Adobe Photoshop depicting
hi-rise blocks ... mentally ill Black people ...
and tortured souls sellin' their bodies for crack.
Dream weaver will not be used to create a website
with images of Afro centric Wannabe's wearing
Kente Cloth ...
tellin' young Urban Warriors about Malcolm 'X'
and pseudo revolutionary Urban politics.
Macromedia Director will not be able to create
a CD Rom about gang members who disregard
the call to lay down arms and take you out by any
means necessary
Designer clothes will not be relevant
We won't care if she slept with her Sisters Boyfriends
Cousin's Brother on Jerry Springer
We won't be bothered how many pieces of Kentucky
Fried Chicken you can get for four pounds ...
No one will be interested in your man ... your 3
baby mothers ...
Fake attitude 'N' American Express smile
Coz terror and its cousin fear will be occupying the streets
The revolution will not be digital
There will be no repeats on News night or Channel
Four News
And we won't give a damn if there's no Black newsreaders
The Spice Girls will not write the musical introduction
Or Boyzone ... It will not be sung by Robbie Williams
Shania Twain ... Elton John or any other fake
Wannabe Black boy band
The revolution shall not return after a commercial break
Party political broadcast
Or a newsflash about corrupt politicians
There will be no subtitles or sign language
There will be no pay per view option
You will not have to worry about

Keeping fit ... Holistic living ...
Healthy eating
Or child care provision
The revolution will not get better with Heroin
The revolution will not stop cancer
The revolution will not care how many stocks and shares
you have
The revolution will not care if you live in the suburbs
The revolution will not care if you go skiing in France
The revolution will not care if you've got a degree
The revolution will not care if you're a vegetarian or
meat eater
The revolution will not care if you're a Christian
Or Jehovah's Witness
You won't be watching from the sidelines
In the stand ... Or the front row
Coz it'll infect you like a rash ... eatin' you alive
The revolution will not be digital
Will not be digital
Not be digital
Be digital
The revolution will be live 'N' direct
And you'll be playin' a starring role
Are you prepared for the digital revolution?

Epilogue

This cultural libation has guided me to a place of safety, confidence, and, more importantly, balance. I have always occupied the binary of 'community' and 'academic space', which are continually suspicious of each other and, at times, are incredibly unsafe places to occupy. Once upon a time, I was quite happy to go along with the surreal nature of university, while at the same time consuming the undiluted passion and rawness of the community in which I resided. However, in these turbulent times, when many people are suffering, where young people are lacking in direction and struggling to find purpose, the urgency to unite these two fractious entities has become increasingly significant. At times this unresolved conflict reminds me of two warring family members who, in spite of being able to justify why they 'don't get on', cannot remember what they were fighting about in the first place. Many things have changed, not least me. The irony of feeling both liberated and trapped in both spaces is at times draining and painful in equal measure. Unable to go back to what I was, yet not yet fully formed in terms of being rebirthed is a strange paradox. Six decades later I have arrived at a new destination, having journeyed through light and dark, sweet and sour, sad and hurtful. Mediocrity has no place in my life. Like a marathon runner, I am poised to begin a long arduous journey where the route is mapped out, but my training has prepared me well. I have met myself for the first time. I am now more philosophical, gaining new wisdom, and have acquired a mind not held captive by oppressive and dark forces. I no longer want to be held captive by biased assumptions, subordination, false consciousness, or to pander to the lowest common denominator. I like smiling, simple pleasures, and finding comfort in doing very little. The bigger picture, which I have been socialized to embrace, has little meaning when I reflect on what really matters – love, family, accepting myself, and generally living in a deeper state of calm.

Provocation

How does the development of a black arts infused criminological imagination as a decolonizing agent within the discipline enhance or impede your personal development as a scholar, lecturer, or student?

Provocation responses

Hopefully at the end of this journey through my book you have drawn conclusions, engaged with the provocations, and are in a new place. Some of you may have been taken aback by the questions, others may have felt a powerful response, whilst other may be dismissive on account of not seeing the relevance. After all, it's only a book. These 11 provocations are what I've been trying to engage criminology, my white colleagues and curriculum developers in for many years. Without a commitment to embed a black art within the discipline, then unfortunately the discipline itself will remain stagnant where the study of the racialization of crime and criminal justice is concerned, further marginalizing another generation who are seeking change, excluding yet a new generation of scholars who are hungry to find new solutions to old problems. The future may be uncertain and full of trepidation, but I'm relieved I have given myself permission to pursue my freedom. Connecting to the art of black criminology and black art may finally enable me to walk off the plantation with a vow never to return.

Thanks for walking with me.

Bibliography

Adams, T.E., Ellis, C. and Jones, S.H. (2017) *The International Encyclopedia of Communication Research Methods* (1–10), Hoboken, NJ: John Wiley and Sons.

Agnew, R. (2006) Storylines As a Neglected Cause of Crime, *Journal of Research in Crime and Delinquency*, 43(2): 119–47.

Agozino, B. (2010) What is Criminology? A Control-Freak Discipline!, *African Journal of Criminology of Criminal Justice Studies*, 4(1): 1–20.

Akbar, N. (1991) *Visions for Black Men*, Tallahassee, FL: Mind Productions.

Akom, A. (2008) Black Metropolis and Mental Life: Beyond the Burden of 'Acting White' – Toward a Third Wave of Critical Racial Studies, *Anthropology & Education Quarterly*, 39(3): 247–65.

Alexander, M. (2010) *The New Jim Crow – Mass incarceration in the Age of Colorblindness*, New York, NY: The New Press.

Allen, R. (2001) *The Concept of Self – A Study of Black Identity and Self-esteem*, Detroit, MI: Wayne State University Press.

Allison, H. (1948) Corollary, *Ellery Queen Mystery Magazine*, 12(56): 84–101.

Alvesson, M. and Skoldberg, K. (2009) *Reflexive Methodology: New Vistas for Qualitative Research*, London: Sage.

Anderson, E. (1990) *Streetwise: Race, Class, and Change in an Urban Community*, New Haven, CT: Yale University Press.

Anderson, E. (1999) *Code of the Street: Decency, Violence, and the Moral Life of the Inner City*, New York, NY: Norton.

Anderson, E. (2015) The White Space, *Sociology of Race and Ethnicity*, 1(1): 10–21.

Asante, M.K. (1987) *The Africentric Idea*, Philadelphia, PA: Temple University Press.

Banton, M. (1987) *Racial Theories*, Cambridge: Cambridge University Press.

Barak, G. (1991) Cultural Literacy and a Multi-Cultural Inquiry into the Study of Crime and Justice, *Journal of Criminal Justice Education*, 2(2): 173–92.

Baraka, A. (2011) The Black Arts Movement, Its Meaning and Purpose, *Journal of Contemporary African Art*, 29: 23–31.

Barnes, S.L., Robinson, Z.F. and Wright, E. (2014) *Repositioning Race: Prophetic Research in a Post Racial Obama Age*, New York, NY: SUNY Press.

Becker, H. (1963) *Outsiders: Studies in Sociology and Deviance*, New York, NY: Free Press.

Bell, D. (1992) *Faces at the Bottom of the Well: The Permanence of Racism*, New York, NY: Basic Books.

Bell, D. (1995) *Critical Race Theory: The Key Writings that Formed the Movement*, New York, NY: The New Press.

Boal, A. (2000) *Theatre of the Oppressed*, London: Pluto.

Bobo, J., Hudley, C. and Michel, C. (2004) *The Black Studies Reader*, New York, NY: Routledge.

Bochner, A. (2014) *Coming to Narrative – A Personal History of Paradigm Changes in the Human Sciences*, Walnut Creek, CA: Left Coast Press.

Bonner, A. and Tolhurst, G. (2002) Insider/Outsider Perspectives of Participant Observation, *Nurse Researcher*, 9(4): 7–19.

Bosworth, M., Bowling, B. and Lee, M. (2008) Globalization, Ethnicity and Racism: An Introduction, *Theoretical Criminology*, 12(3): 263–73.

Bowling, B. and Phillips, C. (2002) *Racism, Crime, and Justice*, London: Longman.

Brown, L. and Strega, S. (2005) *Research as Resistance: Critical, Indigenous, and Anti-Oppressive Approaches*, Toronto: Canadian Scholars Press.

Brown, W. (2013) An Intersectional Approach to Criminological Theory: Incorporating the Intersectionality of Race and Gender into Agnew's General Strain Theory, *Supreme Court's Adjudication on Section IV of the Voting Rights Act of 1965*, 4(1): 1–15.

Browning, S. and Cao, L. (1992) The Impact of Race and Criminal Justice Ideology, *Justice Quarterly*, 9(4): 685–701.

Bruce, J.E. (1908) *The Black Sleuth*, Boston, MA: North Eastern University Press.

Carbado, D.W. and Roithmayr, D. (2014) Critical Race Theory Meets Social Science, *Annual Review of Law and Social Science*, 10: 149–67.

Carr, W. and Kemmis, S. (1986) *Becoming Critical: Education, Knowledge and Action Research*, Lewes: Falmer Press.

Carrabine, E. (2016) Changing Fortunes: Criminology and the Sociological Condition, *Sociology*, 50(5): 847–62.

Carrington, K., Hog, R. and Sozzo, M. (2016) Southern Criminology, *The British Journal of Criminology*, 56(1): 1–20.

Cashmore, E. (1997) *The Black Cultural Industry*, London: Routledge.

Chang, H. (2008) *Auto Ethnography as Method*, Walnut Creek, CA: Left Coast Press.

Chilisa, B. (2012) *Indigenous Research Methodologies*, London: Sage.

Choo, H. and Ferree, M. (2010) Practising Intersectionality in Sociological Research: A Critical Analysis of Inclusions, Interactions, and Institutions in the Study of Inequalities, *Sociological Theory*, 28(2): 129–49.

Clark, K. (1965) *Dark Ghetto – Dilemmas in Social Power*, New York, NY: Harper and Row.

Colvin, S. (2015) Why Should Criminology Care About Literary Fiction? Literature, Life Narratives and Telling Untellable Stories, *Punishment & Society*, 17(2): 211–29.

Connell, R.W. (2003) *Masculinities*, Cambridge: Polity Press.

Conquergood, D. (2013) *Cultural Struggles: Performance, Ethnography, Praxis*, Ann Arbor, MI: University of Michigan Press.

Counsell, C. and Wolf, L. (2001) *Performance Analysis: An Introductory Coursebook*, London: Routledge.

Covington, J. (1995) Racial Classification in Criminology: The Reproduction of Racialised Crime, *Sociological Forum*, 10(4): 547–68.

Crawford, M.N. (2017) *Black Post Blackness: The Black Arts Movement and Twenty First Century Aesthetics*, Champaign, IL: University of Illinois Press.

Crenshaw, K. (1999) Mapping the Margins: Intersectionality, Identity Politics, and Violence Against Women of Color, *Stanford Law Review*, 43(6): 1241–99.

Cruse, H. (1967) *The Crisis of the Negro Intellectual*, New York, NY: Quill.

Cunneen, C. (2011) Postcolonial Perspectives for Criminology. In: Bosworth, M. and Hoyle, C. (eds) *What Is Criminology?*, Oxford: Oxford University Press, pp 249–66.

Cunneen, C. and Tauri, J. (2016) *Indigenous Criminology*, Bristol: Policy Press.

Curry, T. (2017) *The Man-Not: Race, Class, Genre, and the Dilemma's of Black Manhood*, Philadelphia, PN: Philadelphia Press.

Dean, J. (2017) *Doing Reflexivity: An Introduction*, Bristol: Policy Press.

Defranz, T.F. and Gonzalez, A. (2014) *Black Performance Theory*, Durham, NC: Duke University Press.

Delgado, R. and Stefancic, J. (2000) *Critical Race Theory: The Cutting Edge*, Philadephia, PA: Temple University Press.

Delgado, R. and Stefancic, J. (2005) *The Role of Critical Race Theory in Understanding Race, Crime, and Justice Issues*, New York, NY: John Jay College.

Denzin, N.K. (2003a) *Performance Ethnography: Critical Pedagogy and the Politics of Culture*, London: Sage.

Denzin, N.K. (2003b) Performing [Auto] Ethnography Politically, *The Review of Education, Pedagogy and Cultural Studies*, 25: 257–78.

Denzin, N.K. (2010) *The Qualitative Manifesto – A Call to Arms*, Walnut Creek, CA: Left Coast Press.

Denzin, N.K. (2014) *Interpretative Autoethnography*, London: Sage.

Denzin, N.K. and Lincoln, Y. (1999) *The Handbook of Qualitative Research*, London: Sage.

Denzin, N. and Giardina, M.D. (2017) *Qualitative Inquiry in Neoliberal Times,* London: Routledge.

Drake, D. and Walters, R. (2017) Deviant Knoweldge. In: Brisman, A., Caribbine, E. and South, N. (eds) *The Routledge Companion to Criminological Theory and Concepts*, Abingdon: Routledge, pp 267–9.

Dubois, W.E.B. (1938) *The Souls of Black Folk,* New York, NY: Norton.

Dunbar, P. (1892) *Lyrics of a Lowly Life*, New York, NY: Citadel Press.

Duneier, M. and Back, L. (2006) Voices From the Sidewalk: Ethnography and Writing Race, *Ethnic and Racial Studies*, 29(3): 543–65.

Ellingson, L. (2017) *Embodiment in Qualitative Research*, Abingdon: Routledge.

Ellison, R. (1947) *Invisible Man*, London: Penguin.

Emirbayer, M. and Desmond, M. (2012) Race and Reflexivity, *Ethnic and Racial Studies*, 35(4): 574–99.

Erikson, E.H. (1950) *Childhood And Society*, London: Vintage.

Fanon, F. (1952) *Black Skin, White Masks*, London: Pluto.

Ferell, J. (2014) Manifesto for a Criminology Beyond Method. In: Jacobsen, M.H. (ed) *The Poetics of Crime: Understanding and Researching Crime and Deviance Through Creative Means*, Abingdon: Routledge, pp 285–302.

Ferell, J., Hayward, K. and Young, J. (2008) *Cultural Criminology*, London: Sage.

Fisher, M. (2012) The Land Still Lies: Handsworth Songs and the English Riots, *Sight and Sound*, London: BFI. https://www.bfi-staging.org.uk/news-opinion/sight-sound-magazine/comment/land-still-lies-handsworth-songs-and-english-riots

Fisher, R. (1932) *The Conjure-Man Dies: A Mystery Tale of Dark Harlem*, New York, NY: Ayer Company Publishers, Inc.

Ford, C. (1999) *The Hero With an African Face*, New York, NY: Bantam Books.

Franklin, A. (2004) *From Brotherhood to Manhood – How Black Men Rescue Their Relationships and Dreams from the Invisibility Syndrome*, New York, NY: Wiley.

Freire, P. (1970) *Pedagogy of the Oppressed*, London: Penguin.

Gabbidon, S. (2007) *Criminological Perspectives on Race and Crime*, New York, NY: Routledge.

Gabbidon, S. and Taylor Greene, H. (2012) *Race and Crime*, London: Sage.

Gabbidon, S., Greene, H. and Wilder, K. (2004) Still Excluded? An Update on the Status of African American Scholars in the Discipline of Criminology and Criminal Justice, *Journal of Research in Crime and Delinquency*, 41(4): 384–405.

Gabbidon, S., Greene, H. and Young, V. (2002) *African American Classics in Criminology and Criminal Justice*, New York, NY: Sage.

Garner, S. (2009) *Racisms: An Introduction*, London: Sage.

Gifford, J. (2013) *Pimping Fictions: African American Crime Literature and the Untold Story of Black Pulp*, Philadelphia, PA: Temple University Press.

Gillespie, M.B. (2006) *Film Blackness: American Cinema and the Idea of Black Film*, Durham, NC: Duke University Press.

Gilroy, P. (1987) *There Ain't No Black in the Union Jack*, London: Routledge.

Gilroy, P. (2008) The Myth of Black Criminality. In: Spasek, B. (ed) *Ethnicity and Crime*, Berkshire: McGraw-Hill Education, pp 113–27.

Glasgow, D. (1980) *The Black Underclass: Poverty, Unemployment and Entrapment in Ghetto Youth*, New York, NY: Vintage Books.

Glynn, M. (2010) *Breaking the Fourth Wall*, London: Winston Churchill Trust.

Glynn, M. (2014) *Black Men, Invisibility, and Desistance from Crime: Towards a Critical Race Theory of Desistance*, London: Routledge.

Glynn, M. (2016) Towards an Intersectional Model of Desistance for Black Offenders, *Safer Communities*, 15(1): 24–32.

Glynn, M. (2019) *Speaking Data and Telling Stories: Data Verbalization for Researchers*, Abingdon: Routledge.

Glynn, M. (2020a) Dunbar was Right. In: Farmer, V.L. and Farmer, E.S.W. (eds) *Critical Race Theory in the Academy*, Charlotte, NC: Information Age Publishing, Inc, pp 535–47.

Glynn, M. (2020b) *Midnight Spiral: A Franklin Mystery*, Birmingham: Algorhythm.

Goffman, E. (1959) *The Presentation of Self in Everyday Life*, London: Penguin.

Green, L. (2010) The Sound of Silence: A Framework for Researching Sensitive Issue or Marginalised Perspectives in Health, *Journal of Research in Nursing*, 16(4): 347–60.

Gunaratham, Y. (2003) *Researching Race and Ethnicity: Methods, Knowledge, and Power*, London: Sage.

Hall, S. (1978) *Policing the Crisis*, London: Macmillan.

Hall, S. (1993) What is the 'Black' in Black Popular Culture? *Social Justice*, 20(1–2): 104–14.

Hare, N. (1973) The Challenge of the Black Scholar. In: Ladner, J. (ed) *The Death of White Sociology*, Baltimore, MD: Black Classic Press, pp 67–77.

Harris, T. (1991) *The Selected Works of Ida B. Wella-Barnett*, New York, NY: Oxford University Press.

Harrison, P.C. (2014) Toward a Critical Vocabulary for African Diaspora Expressivity, *The Journal of African Diaspora Drama*, Theatre and Performance, 1(1): 1–14.

Hartney, C. and Vuong, L. (2009) *Created Equal: Racial and Ethnic Disparities in the US Criminal Justice System*, US: National Council on Crime and Delinquency.

Hill-Collins, P. (2000) *Black Feminist Thought*, New York, NY: Routledge.

Hill-Collins, P. (2005) *Black Sexual Politics: African Americans, Gender and the New Racism*, New York, NY: Routledge.

Himes, C. (1975) *Black on Black: Baby Sister and Selected Writings*, London: Michael Joseph Ltd.

Home Office (2006) *Young Black People and the Criminal Justice System*, London: Blackwell Systems.

hooks, b. (1991) *Yearning – Race, Gender, and Cultural Politics*, Boston, MA: South End Press.

hooks, b (2004) *We Real Cool: Black Men and Masculinity*, New York, NY: Routledge.

Hopkins, P. (1901) *Hagar's Daughter: A Story of Southern Caste Prejudice*, Boston, MA: Colored American Magazine.

Hutchinson, E.O. (1994) *The Association of Black Male Image*, New York, NY: Simon & Schuster.

Jacobsen, M.H. (2014) *The Poetics of Crime: Understanding and Researching Crime and Deviance Through Creative Means*, Abingdon: Routledge.

Jones, L. (1963) *Blues People: Negro Music in White America*, New York, NY: William Morrow and Company.

Kitwana, B. (2002) *The Hip-Hop Generation: Young Blacks and the Crisis in African American Culture*, New York, NY: Perseus Books.

Kodwo, E. (2003) Further Considerations on Afrofuturism, *CR: The New Centennial Review*, 3(2): 287–302.

Kutner, R. (1967) *Race and Modern Science*, New York, NY: Social Science Press.

Ladner, J.A. (1973) *The Death of White Sociology, Essays on Race and Culture*, Baltimore, MD: Black Classic Press.

Lammy, D. (2017) *The Lammy Review: An Independent Review into the Treatment of, and Outcomes for, Black, Asian and Minority Ethnic Individuals in the Criminal Justice System*, London: Home Office.

Lawrence, K.O. (2011) *Race, Crime and Punishment in America: Breaking the Connection in America*, Washington, DC: The Aspen Institute.

Liamputtong, P. (2010) *Performing Qualitative Cross-Cultural Research*, Cambridge: Cambridge University Press.

Lombardo, R. (2002) The Black Mafia: African-American Organized Crime in Chicago 1890–1960, *Crime, Law & Social Change*, 38: 33–65.

Lorde, A. (1984) *Sister Outsider*, London: Penguin Classics.

Lynch, M.J. (2000) The Power of Oppression: Understanding the History of Criminology as a Science of Oppression, *Critical Criminology*, 9(1): 144–52.

Lynn, M. (2005) Critical Race Theory, Afrocentricity, and Their Relation to Critical Pedagogy. In: Leonardo, Z. (ed) *Critical Pedagogy and Race*, Malden, MA: Blackwell Publishing, pp 127–40.

Mann, C.R. (1984) *Female Crime and Delinquency*, Tuscaloosa, AL: University of Alabama Press.

Marable, M. (1995) *Beyond Black and White: Transforming African American Politics*, London: Verso.

Marable, M. (2001) Black Studies and the Racial Mountain, *Souls*, 2(3): 17–36.

Marriot, D. (2005) *On Black Men*, Edinburgh: Edinburgh University Press.

Maruna, S. (2001) *Making Good – How Ex-convicts Reform and Rebuild Their Lives*, Washington, DC: APA.

Maruna, S. (2010) Reentry as a Rite of Passage, *Punishment and Society*, 1: 1–26.

Maruna, S. and Immarigeon, R. (2004) *After Crime and Punishment*, Cullompton: Willan Publishing.

Maruna, S. and Roy, K. (2006) Amputation or Reconstruction? Notes on the Concept of 'Knifing Off' and 'Desistance', *Crime Journal of Contemporary Criminal Justice*, 22 (2): 1–21.

Mauer, M. (1999) *Race To Incarcerate*, New York, NY: The New Press.

Mauthner, N.S. and Doucet, A. (2003) Reflexive Accounts and Accounts of Reflexivity in Qualitative Data Analysis, *Sociology*, 37(3): 413–31.

McAdams, D.P. (1985) *Power, Intimacy, and the Life Story*, London: Guildford Press.

McCoy, M.P. (1999) *Black Picket Fences: Privilege and Peril Among the Black Middle Class*, Chicago, IL: University of Chicago Press.

McGregor, R. (2020) Criminological Fiction: What Is It Good For? *Journal of Theoretical & Philosophical Criminology*, 12 (January): 18–36.

Mills, C.W. (1959) *The Sociological Imagination*, New York, NY: Oxford University Press.

Ministry of Justice (2020) *Tackling Racial Disparity in the Criminal Justice System: 2020 Update*, London: Ministry of Justice.

Monroe, N.W. (1900) Crime Among the Negroes of Chicago: A Social Study, *American Journal of Sociology*, 6(2): 204–23.

Mordhorst, M. (2008) From Counterfactual History to Counternarrative History, *Management and Organisational History*, 3(1): 5–26.

Moses, E.R. (1936) Community Factors in Negro Delinquency, *The Journal of Negro Education*, 5(2): 220–27.

Motley, W. (1947) *Knock on Any Door*, Chicago, IL: Northern Illinois University Press.

Neal, L. (1968) The Making of African American Identity, The Black Arts Movement, *National Humanities Center Resource Toolbox*, III: 1–2.

O'Brien, E.L. (2008) *Crime in Verse: The Poetics of Murder in the Victorian Era*, Columbus, OH: Ohio State University Press.

Oliver, W. (1989) Black Males and Social Problems: Prevention through Afrocentric Socialization, *Journal of Black Studies*, 20(1): 15–39.

Olusoga, D. (2016) *Black and British: A Forgotten History*, London: MacMillan.

Neuman, M. (1996) Collecting Ourselves at the End of the Century. In: Ellis, C. and Bochner, A. (eds) *Composing Ethnography: Alternative Forms of Qualitative Writing*, London: Alta Mira Press, pp 172–98.

Parham, T. (1989) Cycles of Psychological Nigrescence, *The Counseling Psychologist*, 17(2): 187–226.

Park-Fuller, L. (2000) Performing Absence: The Staged Personal Narrative as Testimony, *Text and Performance Quarterly*, 20: 20–42.

Parmar, A. (2016) Race, Ethnicity and Criminal Justice: Refocussing the Criminological Gaze. In: Bosworth, M., Hoyle, C. and Zedner, L. (eds) *Changing Contours of Criminal Justice*, Oxford: Oxford University Press, pp 55–69.

Patel, T. and Tyrer, D. (2011) *Race, Crime, and Resistance*, London: Sage.

Paternoster, R. and Bushbay, S. (2009) Desistance and the 'Feared Self': Toward an Identity Theory of Criminal Desistance, *Journal of Criminal Law and Criminology*, 99(4): 1103–56.

Peaker, A. (1998) *Nuff Respect: The Creative and Rehabilitative Needs of Black Offenders*, Loughborough: The Unit for Arts and Offenders.

Penzler, O. (2009) *Black Noir: Mystery, Crime and Suspense Fiction by African American Writers*, New York, NY: Pegasus Press.

Petersilia, J. (2001) Prisoner Re-entry: Public Safety and Reintegration Challenges, *The Prison Journal*, 81(3): 360–75.

Petry, A. (1946) *The Street*, New York, NY: Houghton Mifflin Harcourt.

Phillips, C. and Bowling, B. (2003) Racism, Ethnicity, and Criminology: Developing Minority Perspectives, *British Journal of Criminology*, 43(2): 269–90.

Phillips, C. and Webster, C. (2014) *New Directions in Race, Ethnicity and Crime*, London: Routledge.

Phillips, C., Earle, R., Parmar, A. and Smith, D. (2020) Dear British Criminology: Where Has All the Race and Racism Gone?, *Theoretical Criminology*, 24(3): 427–44.

Pietila, A. (2010) *Not in My Neighbourhood*, Chicago, IL: Ivan R. Dee.

Pinnock, D. (1997) *Gang Rituals and Rites Of Passage*, South Africa: Africa Sun Press.

Polk, K. (1999) Males and Honor Contest Violence, *Homicide Studies*, 2(1): 6–29.

Presser, L. and Sandberg, S. (2015) *Narrative Criminology: Understanding Stories of Crime*, New York, NY: NYU Press.

Pryce, K. (1979) *Endless Pressure*, London: Penguin.

Ramdarshan, M. (2019) *Representation of People of Colour Among Children's Book Authors and Illustrators*, London: BookTrust.

Rich, J. (2009) *Wrong Place, Wrong Time: Trauma and Violence in the Lives of Young Black Men*, Baltimore, MD: Johns Hopkins University Press.

Richey-Mann, C. (1984) *Female Crime and Delinquency*, Tuscaloosa, AL: University of Alabama Press.

Robinson, G. (1919) Music and Crime, *The Journal of Education*, 89(18): 485–6.

Russell, K. (2002) Development of a Black Criminology: The Role of the Black Criminologist. In: Gabbidon, S., Greene, H. and Young, V. (eds) *African American Classics in Criminology and Criminal Justice*, New York: Sage, pp 667–83.

Russell-Brown, K. (2002) *The Colour of Crime*, New York, NY: Sage.

Russell-Brown, K. (2019) Black Criminology in the 21st Century. In: Unnever, J.D., Gabbidon, S.L. and Chouy, C. (eds) *Building a Black Criminology*, New York, NY: Routledge, pp 101–23.

Saldana, J. (2005) *Ethno-Drama – An Anthology of Reality Theatre*, New York, NY: Rowman and Littlefield.

Saldana, J. (2009) *The Coding Manual for Qualitative Researchers*, London: Sage.

Saldana, J. (2011) *Ethnotheatre: From Page to Stage*, Walnut Creek, CA: Left Coast Press.

Saleh-Hanna, V. (2010) Crime, Resistance and Song: Black Musicianship's Black Criminology, *Sociology of Crime, Law and Deviance*, 14: 145–71.

Sampson, R.J. and Lauritsen, J.L. (1997) Racial and Ethnic Disparities in Crime and Criminal Justice in the United States, *Crime and Justice*, 21: 311–74.

Sampson, R.J. and Wilson, J. (1995) *Toward a Theory of Race, Crime, and Urban Inequality*, Palo Alto, CA: Stanford University Press.

Sampson, R., Wilson, W. and Katz, H. (2018) Reassessing 'Toward a Theory of Race, Crime, and Urban Inequality': Enduring and New Challenges in 21st Century America, *Du Bois Review: Social Science Research on Race,* 15(1): 13–34. doi:10.1017/S1742058X18000140.

Sentencing Project (2008) *Reducing Racial Disparity in the Criminal Justice System: A Manual for Practitioners and Policymakers*, Washington, DC: The Sentencing Project.

Serrant-Green, L. (2010) The Sound of Silence: A Framework for Researching Sensitive Issue or Marginalised Perspectives in Health, *Journal of Research in Nursing*, 16(4): 347–60.

Siegal, L. and Zalmon, M. (1991) Cultural Literacy in Criminal Justice: A Preliminary Assessment, *Journal of Criminal Justice Education*, 2(1): 15–44.

Solorzano, D. and Yosso, T. (2002) Critical Race Methodology: Counterstorytelling as an Analytical Framework, *Qualitative Inquiry*, 8(1): 23–44.

Spence, L. (2010) White Space, Black Space, *The Urbanite*, 68: 43–5.

Spry, T. (2001) Performing Autoethnography: An Embodied Methodological Praxis, *Qualitative Inquiry*, 7(6): 706–32.

Staples, R. (1960) White Racism, Black Crime, and American Justice: An Application of the Colonial Model to Explain Crime and Race, *Phylon*, 36(1): 14–22.

Thompson, J. (1998) *Prison Theatre: Perspectives and Practices*, London: Jessica Kingsley Publishers.

Thornberry, T. (1990) Cultural Literacy in Criminology, *Journal of Criminal Justice Education*, 1(1): 33–49.

Tierra, A. de la and Henne, K. (2017) Southern Theory. In: Brisman, A., Caribbine, E. and South, N. (eds) *The Routledge Companion to Criminological Theory and Concepts*, Abingdon: Routledge, pp 381–5.

Tonry, M. (2011) *Punishing Race: A Continuing American Dilemma*, Oxford: Oxford University Press.

Travis, J., McBride, E. and Solomon, A. (2005) *Families Left Behind: The Hidden Costs of Incarceration and Re-entry*, Washington, DC: Urban Institute.

Turner, V. (1969) *The Ritual Process: Structure and Anti-Structure*, New York, NY: De Gruyter.

Ugwu, C. (1995) *Let's Get It On: The Politics of Black Performance*, Seattle, WA: Bay Press.

United Nations (1997) *Caribbean Social Structures and the Changing World of Men*, CDCC, United Nations.

Unnever, J.D. and Gabbidon, S.L. (2011) *A Theory of African American Offending – Race, Racism, and Crime*, New York, NY: Routledge.

Unnever, J.D., Gabbidon, S.L. and Chouy, C. (2019) *Building a Black Criminology: Race, Theory, and Crime*, New York, NY: Routledge.

Valdes, F., Culp, J. and Harris, A. (2002) *Crossroads, Directions and a New Critical Race Theory*, Philadelphia, PA: Temple Press.

Webster, C. (2007) *Understanding Race and Crime*, Maidenhead: Open University Press.

West, C. (1993) *Race Matters,* Boston, MA: Beacon Press.

Wilson, A. (1994) *Black on Black Violence*, New York, NY: Afrikan World Info Systems.

Woods, P.L. (1996) *Spooks, Spies, and Private Eyes: An Anthology of Black Mystery, Crime and Suspense Fiction of the 20th Century*, Edinburgh: Payback Press.

Young, J. (2011) *The Criminological Imagination*, Cambridge: Polity Press.

Zamudo, M., Russell, C., Rios, F. and Bridgeman, J. (2011) *Critical Race Theory Matters: Education and Ideology*, London: Routledge.

Zinn, H. (1959) *Race*, New York, NY: Seven Stories Press.

Zoboi, I. and Salaam, Y. (2020) *Punching the Air*, London: Harper Collins.

Index